Gracefully

Looking and Being Your Best at Any Age

VALERIE RAMSEY

WITH

HEATHER HUMMEL

New York Chicago San Francisco Lisbon London Madrid Mexico City
Milan New Delhi San Juan Seoul Singapore Sydney Toronto

The McGraw·Hill Companies

Library of Congress Cataloging-in-Publication Data

Ramsey, Valerie.
     Gracefully : looking and being your best at any age / by Valerie Ramsey with
Heather Hummel.
          p.   cm.
     Includes index.
     ISBN 978-0-07-154623-2 (alk. paper)
          1. Life skills—Handbooks, manuals, etc.   2. Aging—Handbooks, manuals, etc.
I. Hummel, Heather.   II. Title.

     HQ2037.R36   2008
     646.7'9—dc22   2007035673

1 2 3   4 5 6 7 8 9 10 11 12 13 14 15 16 17 18 19 20 21   FGR/FGR   0 9 8

ISBN 978-0-07-154623-2
MHID   0-07-154623-5

Interior design by Susan H. Hartman
Photographs on part openers and Chapters 2, 3, 4, 5, 9, 10, 11, 12, 13, 14, 15 copyright
© by Deidre Fuller; on Chapter 1 copyright © by Tom O'Neal; on Chapter 6 copyright © by
Bill Janes; on Chapter 7 copyright © by Rick Pharaoh; on Chapter 8 copyright © by Roberto
Ligresti; on Chapters 16, 17 from the personal collection of the author; on Chapter 18
copyright © by Barnaby Draper

McGraw-Hill books are available at special quantity discounts to use as premiums and
sales promotions or for use in corporate training programs. To contact a representative,
please visit the Contact Us pages at www.mhprofessional.com.

The information contained in this book is intended to provide helpful and informative
material on the subject addressed. It is not intended to serve as a replacement for
professional medical advice. Any use of the information in this book is at the reader's
discretion. The author and publisher specifically disclaim any and all liability arising
directly or indirectly from the use or application of any information contained in this book.
A health care professional should be consulted regarding your specific situation.

This book is printed on acid-free paper.

 To Mima

Contents

Part 2 *The Mind*

Part 3 *The Soul*

Foreword

Susan Lucci

We are not meant to live our lives bathed in fear and doubt. We are meant to embrace life's moments as they unfold. Each unfolding ought to be treated as a gift, a lesson, or a pleasure. I share in Valerie's philosophy of combining body, mind, and soul to create our dreams and to always look to the next chance to make a new dream come true.

It was a few years ago, when I was filming a segment for "Entertainment Tonight" at Pebble Beach, that I first met Valerie. Valerie and her husband, Wally, joined my husband, Helmut, and me for dinner, where we shared stories about New York City. Enchanted by the Scottish bagpipers who played at sundown on the greens of Spanish Bay, Helmut and I decided to stay one more night—one of many examples of embracing life in the moment when our busy schedule permits.

Whether you're in your twenties or sixties or nineties, my conviction is to never believe, think, or act as though you are old. In fact, take the word *old* out of your vocabulary! Life gives us many chances to conceptualize and live our dreams, but if we are too busy shadowing these possibilities with fear of aging, then they may slip away. The alternative is so much sweeter.

Along the way, share your journey, as Valerie is doing with this book, and learn that by inspiring others, we continue to inspire ourselves, to shine, and to allow wonderful events to unfold.

Valerie, like me, believes that by staying physically, mentally, and spiritually fit, we are better prepared for our own individual adventure. Inner beauty resonates as outer beauty. Think about it: the most beautiful women are those who put a smile on others' faces with their own smile, yet a frown on the most stunning woman is still a frown.

Valerie's message on the pages of this book will inspire you to live life without limitations. Everyone has a dream, and it doesn't have to be about acting or modeling. It is about what makes you as an individual whole and happy.

Preface

Traveling by plane can either be terrifying or exhilarating—or both! All the same, when the plane reaches an altitude of thirty-five thousand feet, everyone aboard is en route to their destination. Some people travel light, with only a small bag in the overhead compartment, while others travel with cumbersome, checked luggage that they will spend time retrieving in baggage claim. While they are suspended in midair, travelers pass the time by working, reading, playing video games, engaging in the in-flight movie, writing postcards, and napping as the plane progresses to its intended destination, where goals, dreams, and a continuance of life await them.

Behind on the runway, there are more planes filled with eager passengers, buckling their seatbelts and awaiting takeoff instructions. The cabin lights are dimmed, the engines roar as the craft gently taxi down their assigned airstrips. Having made it through the gate and boarding sequence, these travelers are soon to be airborne, knowing they are moving forward.

Meanwhile, back at the terminal, the gates and passageways teem with new travelers with different agendas and itineraries. Some stand with glazed eyes, scanning the boards that list so many flights. Others wrestle words with the ticket counter employees over seat assignments and missed or canceled flights. Still others hold on to their tickets for dear life, afraid to board their flights, on the verge of turning back to the parking garage. Then there are those who sit at a gate and simply wait. They wait for their plane to arrive, for the flight attendant to tell them when their flight will leave. These travelers are the saddest of all, because they sit and wait as other people full of angst, excitement, fear, and intention, with tickets in hand, pass by and continue with their agendas.

Take a moment and put yourself into this scenario. If it were a reflection of your life, where would you be? Are you on the plane that is already in flight? Aboard the plane waiting for clearance on the runway? In the terminal staring in a fog at the choices on the flight board? Or are you the one who sits and waits for someone to dictate a destination for you?

If you saw yourself on the flight that was airborne, you might just be sitting next to Valerie Ramsey and others who are continuing to chase their dreams and explore new territory. Throughout this book, Valerie takes you as her personal guest aboard the flight that carried her from a childhood spent primarily in boarding schools to her role as a stay-at-home mother to my five siblings and me, then to a career in public relations for one of the top resorts in the world, and finally to her latest role as a runway, commercial, and print model at the age of sixty-three. Now sixty-eight, she holds the titles of mother to six (parenting never ends!), grandmother to seven (at the time of this writing), public relations manager, and fashion model.

Valerie goes into great personal detail about the art of aging gracefully. She shares her formulas, tips, and advice for being the best you can be at any age. Backed by professionals in the industry, she will inspire you to follow your own itinerary and to find your way out of the chaos of the terminal to the plane that is flying forward. She leads by example, not a cast-iron mold, encouraging you to embark on new journeys that are meant to create and keep balance between your body, mind, and soul and to further your spiritual, emotional, and physical growth. When you are inspired by others, the gift of learning, experiencing, and finding your own destination evolves.

Valerie's and my wish for you is that with this book, you will find or continue to pursue your goals and dreams in manners that manifest in truly remarkable ways through beauty and grace.

—Heather Hummel

Acknowledgments

Team effort—without it, this book would never have been possible. Appreciation— words cannot begin to express the depth of my feelings, but I'd like to try, knowing that I am only touching the surface of the gratitude that fills me. First and foremost, to my beautiful daughter Heather Hummel, who initially came up with the idea of writing *Gracefully* and was so tireless in her pursuit of its publication. Although its writing was a joint effort, without her, it never would have come about. Her grandmother would be extraordinarily proud.

Both Heather and I would like to express our immense appreciation to our literary agents, Olga Vezeris and Jackie Meyer of Whimsy, LLC, for their immediate support of and vision for this project; and to John Aherne, our editor, for his tremendous enthusiasm for what *Gracefully* is all about and for all of his expertise in guiding us through to its completion; to art director Tom Lau; to our publicist, Sandi Shands; to editorial assistant Joseph Berkowitz; and to editing, design, and production supervisor Julia Anderson Bauer, copyeditor Karen Steib, designer Susan H. Hartman, prepress artist Pamela Juarez, and proofreader Sharon Honaker, and the entire team at McGraw-Hill for their wonderful creativity and sense of what would be exactly right. A very special thank you to Lynn Goldberg, Grace McQuade, and Kathleen Carter of

Goldberg McDuffie, who were so incredibly passionate about this project from the moment we walked into their offices. You have been invaluable to our team.

Acknowledgment and great appreciation also go to my gracious friend, Susan Lucci, for contributing the foreword to this book. If ever there was a role model, Susan is certainly it.

Appreciation on a grand scale to all the others who made up our team with their generous contributions of both time and expertise: Dr. Arlene Noodleman, Derek Johnson, Olave Menczkowski, Jeffery Hasseler, John Cecalupo, and Darren Dyck.

My love and gratitude go out to my daughter Paula Anne, who was an invaluable help with designing and maintaining my website and to my daughter Darcy for creating my workout routine and helping to keep me physically fit! Thank you also to the rest of my children—Jim, Gus, and Katy—and to all of my beautiful grandchildren—Kristin, P.J., Jack R., Lauren and Jack L., and Alex and Jennifer. You light up my life every day. To my husband, Wally, for your love, support, and firm belief in Heather and me and in this book, and for your divine patience with all the hours spent at my computer—thank you. I couldn't have done this without you.

I would like to acknowledge with gratitude and appreciation the many special friends who showed their support throughout this project, beginning with David Krieff, the "Hollywood producer who first 'discovered' me"; Jim Bell, executive producer of the "Today Show"; Reed Grinsell of "Extra"; Jan Wahl of KRON-TV; Erin Clark of KSBW-TV; David Anderson of Ford Chicago; Larry Bloustein and Lynn Plage; photographers Deidre Fuller, Tom O'Neil, Bill Janes, and Rick Pharoah; and the freelance writers and promoters who made my story known—Brenda Moore and Mike Hale of the *Monterey County Herald*, Glen Putman, Stephanie Lingle

Beasley, Glenn Newman, Marty Lewis, Ray Napolitano, and Anita Jaffe.

Family and friends are the glue that enrich every day and bring so much meaning to our lives. Special love and thanks to friends Gordon and Peggy Hahn, our annual traveling companions with whom we have shared hundreds, if not thousands, of adventures and laughs. Other treasured friends I would like to thank for being cheerleaders in my life and throughout this project are Fritz Trask, John and Diane Boynton, Bev James, Mary Grace Richheimer, Katy Brown, Margie and Bill Ely, George and Katherine Crispo, Ken and Daria Dolan, Laurie Dhue, Joe and Jean Ravalese, Marisa Fox, Noel Castellanos, Cyndy Spengler, Ted and Velma Balestreri, Bert and Bella Cutino, Roxanne Wilde, Pam Carroll, Darcy Blackburn, Sylvia Bliskak, Molly Joest, Sunday Spencer, Reverend Lorenzo Robinson, and my good friends at Murphy O'Brien Communications—Karen Murphy O'Brien, Stacy Lewis, Pieter Ruig, and Meredith Seacrest.

I also want to give warm thanks to Margie Quattrochi, all of my wonderful friends at Tiffany & Co., and Terry Tiffany. Your friendship and enthusiastic support have meant the world to me.

Chapter 16 was written in memory of two very dear friends, Anne Griswold and Melissa Trask. Wally and I were deeply saddened to have lost them this year. Their spirit and love fill our hearts.

And finally, a very warm and special thanks to Pebble Beach Resorts. I have truly loved and enjoyed every single day I have spent in this magnificent setting and have deeply appreciated being so fortunate as to work at one of the most beautiful properties in the world. During my time here, I have met extraordinary people and have had experiences beyond my wildest dreams. Thank you.

—Valerie Ramsey

Great wealth is found in the friendships we cultivate and with the people who enrich our lives. My deepest gratitude goes to those who have shown me the definition of true friendship through their love, actions, words, and support. I raise my glass (or my pen) to you: Susan Erickson, my soul sister; Mitzi Santana for simply listening; Carrie Smith for always being there; Crystal and Nathan Newell for loving and caring for my pups; Amy Taylor for inadvertently bringing my pups into my life; Robin Fredner for keeping the Volvo in running order and my pups well cared for during my travels. And to those who have been my friends and/or support system over the years: Ken and Tyler Dederick, Tanya Brockett, Ginny Moran, Laura Scheinder and family, Susan Schwartz, Nan Khayatt, Wistar Murray, Jeff and Adriana Haynes, Bill Rudd, Howard Barnett, Jonathan Coleman, Martin St. George, Walt Markey, William Guilford, Charlotte Baecher, Tom Castner, Barbara Glynn, Kristin Otto, Carl Otto, Todd Hughes, and Eric Wilson. A very special thank you to Dr. Kathryn Ehlers.

My appreciation to Donna Plasket; Jennifer Newell; the faculty, students, alumni, and the team of professionals of the University of Virginia's Bachelor of Interdisciplinary Studies program.

To Doug Ellis, photographer extraordinaire, for capturing both of my good sides.

To Fred and Darcy Scott and family, who paid me my first hard-earned dollar, and to Amanda Leahy—our friendships have aged better than fine wine.

To Middle Carr who, whether it was over "coffee" at Barnes & Noble or sitting at the wine bar, saw me through the writing process with unwavering belief and loud cheers. You are a true artist when it comes to the art of friendship.

Julie, Stephan, and Gabriel—the three of you keep me grounded and laughing! No words can describe the meaning you have in my life.

My warmest gratitude to Toan Nguyen of C'ville Coffee, who not only fed me well (the best "Honey Bunches" and chocolate chip cookies!) as I wrote chapter after chapter, but who, along with Ross Bishop, made going to the "office" a wonderful experience. I love you guys!

This book's dedication is to "Mima"—my grandmother, Dorothy Crispo—who was my first "editor" and has always been my role model and guardian angel. Thank you, Mima, for your love, guidance, and the P1800!

And last, to my father, who during my youth sat at the kitchen table with me, going over my essays with love and a red pen. And to my mother who has always shown her family how to live gracefully.

—Heather Hummel

Part 1

The Body

Chapter 1

Fit, Young, and Vital

There is a fountain of youth: it is your mind, your talents, the creativity you bring to your life and the lives of people you love. When you learn to tap this source, you will truly have defeated age.

—*Sophia Loren*

From the moment we are born, we begin growing in all aspects of life—mental, physical, and spiritual. As children, we are barely aware that this is taking place. By the time we reach our teens, we think we know all there is to know about life—or at least all we want to know. We quickly realize the folly of this attitude as we enter adulthood and life continues to challenge and cajole us into more growth.

Our twenties are spent exploring life with a youthful, free-spirit attitude filled with wide-eyed, sometimes naive dreams of the future. Some of us delve into careers, others travel, and still others marry and start families.

By the time we reach our thirties, we've usually learned—sometimes the hard way—that we will always continue to grow. We've experienced enough love and loss by then to acknowledge, and even start to respect, that there is such a thing as wisdom that comes with age.

Our forties give us the chance to start looking back on our lives while still striding confidently into the future. We consider the choices we have made and, if given the opportunity, whether we would make them again. For those we wouldn't change, we are eternally grateful. For those we would like to do something about, we still have the strength and vision to plan a new course.

This trend continues into our fifties and beyond. By our "golden years" we may have moved to a new town, our kids may have moved out and established busy careers and lives of their own, and we might be grandparents. Retirement nudges the back of our minds, and we wonder if we've planned well enough. We look forward to easing into a long and relaxing retirement, surrounded by family and friends. Sound familiar?

Most of what I've described is what some might consider the "typical" ebb and flow of life. Then there are people who live life according to another plan, as I have. Either by choice, circumstance or both, we veer onto a less traditional course at some point in our lives. After spending most of my youth at boarding school, I followed the conventions of society by marrying in my early twenties, as most people did in the 1950s and 1960s, and starting a family. I mistakenly thought I was at the peak of my fitness, youth, and vitality back then. After dedicating three decades to raising a large family—something I enjoyed very much—I made a drastic turn off the traditional path. It's not that I was rebelling—quite the opposite, in fact. I chose to embrace a different kind of life than the one I had been living.

I did things out of sequence compared to most, in reverse order. I entered the corporate world at age fifty-three, when many women are planning when and how to get out, and I began a modeling career at sixty-three, when most are planning what to wear to their retirement dinners. Prior to that, I had been a stay-at-home mom with six bright and energetic children. Typically, models (and pro athletes) start their careers early in life and then build a second career that is more socially acceptable once they are past their "prime," at which time they may settle down and start a family. There aren't many who raise children first, climb the corporate ladder at midlife, and then turn to modeling as senior citizens.

As you'll read in these pages, my choices and some unexpected acts of grace have made me rethink what the "prime" years of my life really are—perhaps it's *not* all downhill after twenty-five—and what it truly means to age gracefully. My goal is to inspire a younger generation to look forward to *all* of the years that lie ahead because we never know what life is going to bring—the best years of life may very well be to come. It's simply not true that we have to look at retirement as the end—we should continue to explore life, challenge ourselves, and look around the corner to see what's next. Some of us are climbing mountains, some are starting new businesses, and some are raising grandchildren or even starting a second family.

To age gracefully has everything to do with our inner attitude and gratitude toward life. It means having curiosity and an inquisitive mind, seeking ways to bring joy and abundance into our own lives and those of others, and being more interested in others than we are in ourselves. Living a fit and vital life is about many things. It has as much to do with our spiritual and intellectual beings as it does our physical bodies. Living an enriched life is the essence of living life to the fullest, and if you can do so with grace, all the better.

The chapters in this book address the fundamentals of feeling fit, young, and vital at every age. They present the most complete and inspiring ways I could find to enhance your outlook on life by enhancing your own body, mind, and soul. You'll find valuable advice on exercise, nutrition, building self-confidence, relationships, spirituality, and self-love—all of which are essential to aging gracefully. I'll encourage you to start a journal if you don't already keep one, and we'll look at different ways to use visualization to manifest wonderful experiences. Every word is meant to encourage you to take delight in the life you're experiencing. You can accomplish more in life than you ever imagined if you use your body, mind, and soul in the positive way in which they are meant to be aligned.

Fit After Fifty

Have you ever noticed that someone who's fit, strong, and healthy has a glow and a confidence that is unmistakable? Let's face it—it's sexy! That kind of glow draws others to you in a stronger, more positive way than a pretty face and good hair ever could.

It's clearly important to remain fit and trim for as many years as possible. Being fit gives you the energy and strength to accomplish not only day-to-day tasks, like schlepping grocery bags or carrying a laundry basket up a flight of stairs, but also to enjoy playing games with your grandchildren or hiking up a mountain. We hear and read about fit people having an easier time fending off disease, depression, and illnesses. Additionally, there are lots of social benefits to a healthy lifestyle, such as being able to join a friend for a game of tennis or take a walk on a beach with your spouse or your dog. Most people who are in good shape tend to stick to a workout routine, which gives them a goal and a purpose when they start their day. Working out increases your heart rate, gets your blood flowing, and revitalizes you. Staying fit throughout your life is one of several ways to enhance your vitality and age gracefully. In fact, the best sweat is due to exercise, not to stress.

A Spell of Youth

From the moment we start to feel or think we look old, we begin chasing Ponce de León's fountain of youth. Before you book a trip to St. Augustine, Florida, consider that you have tools of your own that you can use. Youth comes in all forms and attitudes. A few adjustments can make a world of difference.

It happens to everyone one day—that moment when you look in the mirror and admit that you now have a reason to consider night cream. You notice new aches and pains, and while you may have been using preventive antiaging potions and lotions for some time, it's inevitable that a wrinkle or a gray hair will break through your defenses. What I've learned is that accepting and working with these changes in yourself, while also making the most of what you still have going for you, is what keeps you young. Accept aging—because we all age—but continue to be thankful for and work with the youthful aspects you've maintained. Your attitude, words, and approach to life can reflect much more youth than smooth skin, no matter what your driver's license says.

Youth really does come in all ages. I know eighty-year-olds whose eyes and smiles sparkle like they just came home from their first date. Their laugh lines are dimmed by the smiles on their faces. On the flip side, I've met twenty-year-olds who look like they've already lived eighty years. For one reason or another, their outlook is dark and dreary even though they still have so much ahead of them.

The evidence that youth is a state of mind is reinforced from person to person and generation to generation. Which side of the coin do you choose to be? A good place to start is to consider how fit, young, and vital you are now.

Vitality and Living Well

If youth is a state of body and mind, vitality is a state of being—of soul. If you wrap yourself in the essence of vitality, youth will follow. Vitality reflects your higher self, and if it runs high within you, you are likely leading a happy, healthy life filled with fun friends of all ages, a healthy relationship, and a career or other mind stimulus that keeps you waking up before the alarm goes off every morning.

Vitality is the essence of your soul; it helps drive who you are and where you're going. When your vitality level runs high, you're able to make friends in a room full of strangers; you can face life's challenges with the inner knowledge that you're always being tested, and when you face and rise above these tests, you grow and move on.

Vitality brings vigor and passion to what and how you do things in life. It may have been what propelled you through college, or it may have been the driving force behind your decision to start your own business. It's likely that vitality has played a role in your accomplishments, because without it, success is almost impossible. A vital woman exudes confidence and inner beauty. She is strong in mind and purpose. She leads a rich and fulfilling life balanced with loving friends and family, activities and interests, and a career (if that's one of her choices).

Wisdom, grace, and self-confidence are some of the characteristics of people we respect and aspire to emulate. I have lived my life inspired by others with these traits. My mother was my main inspiration—beautiful, graceful, smart, and cosmopolitan in her own right. Having healthy role models in all areas of your life allows you to discover through others the qualities that you want to have, while also allowing you to define what these qualities mean to you personally. Role models are guides for you to observe and learn from; however, they do not set rules. The mentors you meet and work with along the way assist in shaping your thoughts, attitudes, and beliefs. They are there when you have questions, when you falter, and mostly when you succeed. You can apply what you learn from your mentors and then develop your own way of thinking, which is what identifies you as an individual.

I have tried to set my own standards for what leads to a fit, young, and vital life. In this book, I'll guide you through my approach to life, and I hope that you'll be inspired to take action in your own way. You, too, can be fit, young, and vital.

Chapter 2

Body Beautiful

T he abdomen is the reason why man does not
easily take himself for a god.

—*Nietzsche*

So you love everything about your
body, right? No? Okay, maybe
if you're like me and just about
everyone I know, there are a few things on your list of things to
change. We all have them. But when we think about our bodies, the first thing we need to consider is that our perception
of ourselves is often different from the way others see us. We
are our own worst critics! The problem is that when we don't
love ourselves, including our bodies, we subconsciously send a
message to others not to love us as well. Whether verbally or
otherwise, disrespecting our bodies damages our self-esteem
and causes others to look at us in a less-than-perfect light.

Over decades—even centuries—what society has labeled
beautiful has changed drastically. Even today, ideas of what
is beautiful vary from culture to culture. Some cultures prize
bodies that are straight and slim; others value curves and volup-
tuousness; in actuality, there is no single universally ideal body
shape. There are only bodies that are healthy, well-nourished,
and beautiful, and those that are not. This is nothing new.

As a model, my goal is to present a healthy body and self-
image, not a soulless waif on a runway. I believe that I bring
a different attitude to my job, one that is much more spiri-

tual and mental than physical. And it works. People's views of modeling are changing, and they are starting to realize that the perfect body doesn't have to be that of an eighteen-year-old; it's the inner person that matters. When people ask me about modeling, I tell them that it's about learning to love my body, faults and all, and to be willing to promote myself despite them. The great thing is, people are starting to get it.

Accepting Our Changing Bodies

I think we can all agree that by age fifty, sixty, or seventy our bodies aren't what they once were. What used to lay flat, smooth, and taut is now rippled, rough, and loose. Skin that was once as supple as a newborn's is now a bit dry and not as resilient. Stretch marks, veins, and age spots speckle skin in places we didn't think possible when we were young. They resemble the lines on a road map, and we can never be sure where they'll end. It used to be "cool" to read the lines on our palms, but now that we have lines in so many other places, those on our palms just blend in and we don't give them credence anymore. And no one warned us about cellulite when we were in high school health and physical education classes.

These changes happen gradually over time, and we can grow to accept and appreciate them. More importantly, we can appreciate how these road maps and rough surfaces came about. Laugh lines represent years of happiness, and sagging stomachs and breasts remind us of the joys of being moms. These are the telltale signs that we've lived and have a history. There's nothing to be ashamed of there. A high school picture shows innocence and hope, whereas pictures from more sea-soned years depict experience and wisdom. I think it's a fair trade, and some of the most beautiful photographs I've seen are of a mature adult cuddling a grandchild—the contrast is the underlying beauty.

～Putting Our Best Feet Forward～

It seems as if I'm always in front of a camera—not only for work but for family photos, reunions with friends or for-mer classmates, graduations, weddings, job-related events, and once every few years, the dreaded driver's license photo. Think about it—when a camera is aimed at us, we immedi-ately become aware of its presence and hence our appearance. We often respond by consciously or subconsciously thinking of the people who may see the picture and striking a pose or "performing" in order to look our best. Interestingly enough, the best pictures are not the ones where our hair is perfect or the photographer took shot after shot to get it just right; they are the ones where we're happy or thinking about someone or something we love when the shutter clicks. This shows that beauty radiates from within.

So why don't we make a habit of presenting ourselves in the best way possible when the camera is not on us? Naturally, having our picture taken makes us immediately aware of what we're wearing, how our hair looks, and whether our makeup is fresh. In the moment that the flash goes off, we are aware of the self-image we are projecting to others—and that should always be an image of confidence.

Making Every Photo Op Your Best

Since my first day of modeling, I've learned quite a few tips about how to pose and what kind of lighting is the most flattering. Consider the following ideas when you're trying to look your best in front of the camera.

- **Lighting.** I can't tell you how critical lighting is to achieving a good result. It can make you look fabulous, or it can transform you into your worst nightmare. Soft, indirect light or shade is always best, but be careful of shadows that let rays of sun hit the tip of your nose.

- **Posture.** Posture is important when you find yourself in front of a camera. For the best results, angle your body to a three-quarter profile. Keep your head up, your shoulders back and relaxed, and your tummy in.

- **Your best side.** It's been scientifically proven that everyone actually does have a "best side" that is more appealing. Studies have shown that we are drawn to people whose faces are more symmetrical and that when our faces are divided, the difference becomes apparent. Take a piece of paper and cover one half of your face, then the other; you'll see which side is better. Or ask your partner or a trusted friend to tell you which is your best side.

❧ **Multiple photos.** When I first started modeling I was amazed to discover that it's not at all unusual for a photographer to shoot a hundred frames to get that one knockout photo. Naturally this isn't the case in informal situations, but it was quite a revelation. The advent of digital photography has been a tremendous boon to the field. What a convenience to hit "delete" when you're not happy with the way a picture turns out. Feel free to ask the photographer to see the digital images before you move on. That way you'll have a good idea of how they turned out. If using a camera with film, make sure to get a few extra shots to better ensure great results!

❧ **Mona Lisa or Julia Roberts.** Whichever smile comes more naturally to you, let it sparkle. Despite a few wrinkles that might creep out, a brilliant smile radiates youth. Think of something that makes you light up with happiness as you look into the lens. Your joyful spirit will translate to the film (or memory card), and you will be very pleased with the way it turns out.

Building Self-Confidence

What comes across in those pictures we love of ourselves when we are truly happy and in the moment is a sense of self-confidence. I'd like to help you boost your self-confidence and present your physical self with pride, because the more positive energy you project, the more others see you as a positive, healthy person and the more you actually become that person. When you feel good about yourself, your overall self-image starts to transform and bodily changes follow.

From lumpy thighs to jiggly arms to rolls in places you didn't think could roll, you probably have a part of your body that you would like to change—or even move to another spot. With the knowledge and tools available today, you can change your body to some degree through diet and exercise, and you can change your look by donning a new wardrobe. But changing your self-image and level of self-confidence isn't as easy.

Self-confidence doesn't come in a nicely wrapped box with a pink bow and your name on it. It took many years of inner work for me to grow into the self-confident woman I am now. When I learned to present myself with pride and self-respect, I found that people responded in kind and respected me. When you see and feel your own inner and outer beauty more often than you criticize yourself, others will begin to praise you more. Once you've made progress with believing in yourself and your own attractiveness, it's hard to turn back and undo that new, beautiful self-image. People will start to notice your progress and the consistent change in your attitude. With time, they will start to see you as a new and improved person.

Making this transition took time for me. I was a tall, gawky teenager. It seemed that I would never grow into my long legs, and all I could see when I looked in the mirror was flaw upon flaw. My hair was too short or too long or too curly, my waist wasn't tiny enough, my feet were too big, and so on. To make matters worse, the all-girls school I went to had dances with neighboring boys' schools, and the boys who were tall enough for me were invariably the geeky ones, while the really cute guys were always five feet eight or five feet nine. If people had told me then that I would one day become a professional model, I would have thought they were totally out of their minds. As I have learned well, life is truly full of surprises.

Saying It with Body Language

One of the easiest ways you can begin to project self-confidence is through body language. Becoming aware of how your body moves and what it says to others is an essential part of becoming beautiful. The next time you're around a group of people, make a mental note of your body language. When you're in a meeting, do you sit up straight or slouch in your seat? Do you cover your mouth when you talk, or are you open and energetic? Do you look down at the floor when you speak to someone, or do you look that person in the eye? While body language sends all sorts of messages as to how you feel about those around you, it also sends a message of how you feel about yourself. Not many (if any) people are completely happy with their bodies. The goal is to be happy *within* your body, to accept it, flaws and all, and to project this happiness to the rest of the world. When you can accomplish this feat, your self-image will soar.

There has been so much research done on the effects of body language that almost everyone is familiar with the general concepts. When you meet people, body language is a big part of the first impression you make. For instance, the way you carry yourself—shoulders back, head high, back straight—lets people know that you're confident. And believe it or not, confidence without arrogance is sexy. When you walk, sit, or stand with pride, you camouflage what you believe to be your lesser qualities and project yourself in a way that others will respond to positively. Looking people in the eye as you offer a warm smile and a firm handshake immediately projects a strong, confident image. This projection is important because you only have that one chance to make a first impression.

Looking the Part

As we age, the lights in department store dressing rooms are naturally less forgiving than they were in our youth. Finding clothes that fit properly can make a world of difference. I go into greater detail about dressing to look your best in Chapter 7, but it's worth mentioning here that the way you dress says a lot about how you feel toward yourself. Experiment when you're shopping and find clothes that make you feel and look your best. There are many segments on daytime television shows, as well as entire network and cable programs, books, and magazines dedicated to showing how to dress for different body types and how to improve and enhance self-image. Clothes can make a tremendous difference in helping you love and accept your body. When you find flattering clothes that fit properly, your whole persona changes and you project your best and most confident self. Dressing right for an occasion allows you to feel prepared rather than insecure, and you can focus on the event with confidence. So many of the old rules about what to wear have changed. Expectations about appropriate attire are often more forgiving than before, but keep in mind that *forgiving* doesn't always mean *lax*.

Admittedly, one of my advantages is my height, but there are both pluses and minuses to standing five feet ten. On the plus side, a few extra pounds go virtually unnoticed; my children were always able to spot me in the aisles of a crowded grocery or department store; and lengthy arms are elegant when punctuated with sinewy hands and fingers—perfect for sparkling bracelets and rings. Yet with every advantage comes potential disadvantages, including some that other people may not realize.

When I reached my peak height of nearly six feet, I often joked that I was "five-feet-twelve-inches tall" because at the time such a height was not considered attractive or feminine. However, anyone who has shopped for pants recently may think that five feet ten is the "new short" based on the "long" sizes now available on the racks. But in the mid-1990s when I started my career, finding dress pants that were long enough was difficult. I'd always worn skirts to circumvent the problem, but I knew that standing on the eighteenth hole of Pebble Beach Golf Links with travel writers or photographers could be cold and windy in the winter, and I'd want to wear pants. As a woman with a thirty-five-inch inseam, this presented a problem. It's one thing to be able to shorten pants that are too long, but it's impossible to add inches to the hem. One of my favorite finds was Banana Republic's khaki pants, which came in long sizes. I still have the original pair in my closet and have yet to find anything that fits better.

Once I had a few good pairs of pants under my belt, so to speak, it was easy to mix and match tops and blazers. My classic look was maintained with the new pants added to my wardrobe, and I stayed warm on the greens in the winter. One thing I'm very careful about is to always wear jackets that have a curvy fit to them—more like a riding jacket and definitely nothing boxy. I have a horror of looking like a straight-up-and-down ironing board. Curves, in a classic style, are definitely my personal best choice.

I have my own look, the style that suits my body and personality. To find yours, you need to take a good look at your own body. Almost all women's magazines have features on dressing to take advantage of your physical assets and work with those parts of your body you're not terribly proud of. Many books and television talk shows cover the topic for women of all ages and budgets. But if you're not always sure what suits you or feel a new look might be in order, why not work with a friend to get an unbiased opinion about your assets and liabilities? Use the information you gather, but don't rely entirely on external sources. Listen to your inner voice to discover what makes you feel most comfortable. Just because prevailing wisdom says that you shouldn't wear a wide belt with a short torso, this doesn't mean that you can't wear a belt that stands out in some way. Choose one that is narrow but accented with interesting hardware. The choice is yours. As the saying goes, "It's all about you."

When you think about it, loving your body is really only secondary to loving your inner self. If you have self-love—in other words, if you believe in and respect yourself—you've gone a long way toward loving your body as a part of your whole being. Sure, we'd all like to have a great shape, but when we're with other people, it isn't their shape we respond to—it's their personality and energy. We all have things we don't like about ourselves (hips, legs, tummy, whatever), and there are all sorts of ways we can address those things, whether it's clothes or diet and exercise. But if we let our energy and inner light shine through, if we are genuinely interested in others and care more about them than we do ourselves, that's what people will relate to—not our tummy that's a little bigger than we'd like or our less-than-perfect hips.

We discuss the idea of loving ourselves in Chapter 14, but I think it's important to include it here as well, because it ties into everything else in this book. We need to put less importance on our real or perceived faults and more emphasis on our real selves. In fact, the two features that consistently rank highest in polls about what's attractive are the eyes and the smile. That should tell us what really makes a body beautiful!

Chapter 3

Let's Get Physical

A sedentary life is the real sin against the Holy
Spirit. Only those thoughts that come by
walking have any value.

—Nietzsche

Seriously, do I look like I enjoy
sweating? Other than chasing six
kids around for a few decades—
arguably a terrific workout—I was never one to exercise, let
alone have a routine; it just wasn't something I enjoyed. However, in the past four years I've actually grown to like etching
a workout routine into my daily schedule. Now that I can see
and feel the benefits from it, I wish I had started a long time
ago. I feel stronger than I did in my younger years, and I have
biceps and shoulder muscles I haven't seen since I lugged tod-
dlers around. The best part is that it really doesn't take much
time, and I find that in some ways it helps me be more effi-
cient with my morning routine. Getting my blood pumping
early (I'm up and at it at 6 A.M.) wakes me up, which helps me
zip through the rest of my morning rituals a bit faster. I usually wake up before my alarm goes off, excited and ready to do
my workout. (Tip: It helps to set your clock radio to upbeat
music!)

The fundamental benefits of becoming and staying physically fit and active have been touted for years. Granted, some of

the advice has changed and been tweaked depending on studies, fads, and other factors, but the underlying message is the same: exercise is good for you. We know that being physically fit combats the downfalls of aging and health deterioration. Exercise creates life-loving endorphins that give us a natural high. It boosts our metabolism and builds muscles that keep our bones and muscles strong. To me, one of the biggest benefits of staying fit is having the endurance to take pleasure in life. Without that extra energy, I wouldn't enjoy playing with my grandchildren, walking on the beach with my husband, or rushing off to a modeling job after a long day at work.

What's the Best Time of Day for a Workout?

Many people find it easier to allocate time later in the day. But remember that fitting a routine in early in the morning may relieve a lot of the pressure and anxiety that can build during the day from knowing in the back of your mind that you still need to go to the gym (or wherever your activity is). You don't want your exercise routine to be a burden or something you don't enjoy. It should be something you look forward to and feel better for having done. If anything, this may sometimes be the only alone time you have during the day. Working out in the morning sets the tone for your day and starts it off better than a cup of coffee.

The top excuse for not working out is lack of time. But as I've already stated, my workout actually allows me to function better and more efficiently throughout the day, so the time I spend exercising in the morning is time well spent. Of course, there is no one simple answer for building a workout routine or fitness activity into your life, as everyone's schedules and lifestyles vary. The most obvious fact is that you simply *have* to want to do it. That's not to say it won't take a while to learn to enjoy it or to endure the initial muscle soreness. It means that when the alarm clock goes off earlier than it used to or you get to bed a bit later than you'd like to, you know that putting in the time to exercise is worth it.

Before You Get Started

A terrific, nonthreatening place to start is to poke around in a bookstore. Yes, shopping! You'll find numerous books and magazines geared toward starting, maintaining, or building an exercise plan. With the myriad of workout choices out there, it's likely you'll find information on one or several options that can work for you. Look through the books and magazines, and read up on what they recommend for beginners and what looks interesting. It could be that you'll have to try a few activities before finding what's right for you—yoga, kickboxing, running, Pilates, swimming, or something else. Some activities will require a membership at a gym; some you can do on your own or with friends. Discuss your choices with your doctor, who may be able to suggest which of them (or what other activity) would be best for you.

 Walking

One of the impetuses for me to begin exercising was being diagnosed with cardiomyopathy, a condition that involves weakening of the heart muscle. My cardiologist was adamant that I take up walking for a minimum of twenty minutes at least three times a week. Not knowing what else to do, I took his advice and found that it's a fun, easy way to start a basic exercise routine, especially if you haven't exercised in a while. Walking is terrific because it's infinitely easier on the joints than jogging or running, and it can be done literally anywhere with nothing more than a pair of properly fitted walking shoes and comfortable attire. My husband, Wally, and I love to walk along the scenic stretch of Carmel Beach. We have several different routes—sometimes along the beach itself, sometimes through the neighborhoods that front it. The houses that overlook the Pacific always have interesting reconstruction going on, which is fun to watch and provides a good distraction.

Free Weights and At-Home Exercises

When the agencies started sending me to modeling auditions, or "go sees" as they're called in the business, I wanted to firm up my arms for those sleeveless and spaghetti-strap tops and dresses, and I realized that walking alone wasn't going to do this for me. After a few weeks of walking or some other low-intensity exercise, you may want to kick it up a notch, to take your exercise regimen to the next level. Although I thought about hiring a personal trainer to help get myself in shape, I was able to consult my eldest daughter, Darcy Ramsey, who is a personal trainer in Greenwich, Connecticut. During one of my East Coast visits, she took me through a workout and put together a simple plan for me to do at home that combined hand weights, push-ups, and crunches. The goal was to use weights not only to tone and strengthen my arms and upper body, but also to help prevent osteoporosis. Weight-bearing exercise is one of the best things we can do to ward off that disease (see Chapter 5). I'm thrilled to be able to share this workout with you.

You should naturally check with your doctor and a certified personal trainer before attempting any of the exercises given in my personal workout plan. They were customized for me and might not be appropriate for you, but they'll give you an idea of my routine and a starting point for developing your own plan.

Valerie's Workout Plan

Even though I had been walking regularly by the time I started modeling, this new career really tested my level of fitness. I hadn't realized going in that it was such a physically demanding venture, even though I knew it required long days of photo shoots and traveling to auditions. Because many of my modeling assignments take place on weekends or during the evening, I rarely had any downtime and thought working out would further deplete my energy. What I learned was that building stamina and strength through exercise increased rather than reduced the endurance I needed to manage two careers. Within weeks of beginning my routine, I noticed a higher level of vitality and endurance, let alone definition.

Side Shoulder Raises
(2 sets of 15 repetitions on each side)
Stand straight and tall with your knees slightly bent, feet about eighteen inches apart, abdominal muscles in. Breathe deeply in coordination with the reps. Hold a weight in each hand, palms facing your thighs. Raise each arm (one at a time) out to the side and stop at shoulder height. I started with five-pound weights, paying close attention to my posture and breathing. I can feel the pull around my waist, which is a nice reminder that something good must be coming from all of this—not just in my arms and shoulders, but in my torso, too.

Front Shoulder Raises
(2 sets of 15 repetitions on each side)
Use the same five-pound weights and maintain the same stance, with knees slightly bent and palms facing backward, and breathe deeply. This time, slowly raise each arm straight out in front of you, palms downward, to shoulder height.

Bicep Curls
(2 sets of 15 repetitions with each arm)
Stand with your feet about eighteen inches (or hip-width) apart, bending your knees slightly. Hold the weights with your palms facing upward and your upper arms tucked to your sides, elbows bent at a right angle.

Slowly curl the weights simultaneously up toward your shoulders. Hold for a moment, and then slowly lower the weights back to a ninety-degree angle.

Overhead Shoulder Presses
(2 sets of 15 repetitions with each arm)
Without putting the weights down after the bicep curls, move straight into the overhead shoulder presses. Keep your abdominal muscles tucked in. With arms to your sides and elbows bent at a right angle, palms facing each other, slowly raise your arms up over your head simultaneously, twisting them outward so your palms end up facing away from each other. Slowly return your arms back down to the starting position. There are different variations to these presses, so again, check with a trainer.

Push-Ups
(2 sets of 15 repetitions)
There are two basic types of push-ups. The first is done while standing about an arm's length from a wall with your feet eighteen inches (or hip-width) apart. With your elbows bent and palms against the wall at shoulder height, push yourself straight out from the wall. Then ease your way back toward the wall again. Keep your back straight and abdominals tight while pushing in both directions.

The second variation is on the floor. Get on your hands and knees, spreading your hands about eighteen inches apart. Keep your back straight and abdominals tight. Slowly bend your arms to lower your face toward the floor, stopping just as your chin is about to touch the floor, or wherever you are comfortable stopping (just don't go all the way down onto the floor). Then use your arms to push yourself back up to the starting position. When you build up strength, you can start moving your knees farther behind you until they aren't on the floor at all and you're supported by your feet instead.

When I first started working out, I was a complete failure at push-ups, so I began doing them standing up and leaning against the wall, one set of fifteen at a time. This is infinitely easier than trying to do them on the floor!

Next I started doing them on my knees, which is still relatively easy. I have to confess that I have not graduated beyond this point, but that's okay. I'm not trying to become a bodybuilder here. Rather than making the exercise more difficult by doing full-fledged push-ups, I have increased my number of reps. This is a good tip for exercising in general: When you feel that your routine is becoming too easy, increase the number of repetitions you do rather than the amount of weight you use or the difficulty factor of the exercise itself.

Knee Raises
(1 set of 15 repetitions with each knee; work up to 3 sets of 15 repetitions)
Lie on your back on the floor with your arms at your sides. Slowly bring your knees up to your chest simultaneously, then slowly lower and straighten them. Hold them straight out for a count of ten before touching your feet back to the floor.

Crunches

(2 sets of 15 repetitions; work up to 30–40 continuous crunches)

Lie on the floor with your hands folded behind your head and your knees bent. Keeping your back straight, raise your upper body off the floor at an angle of about forty-five degrees, or as far as you can go, as though you are trying to touch your forehead to your knees. Hold this position for a few seconds and then return to the floor. I sometimes do three sets of these if my tummy doesn't feel as flat as I'd like it to.

Jumping Jacks

(20 to 30 continuous)

You can do these just like you did back in gym class. Jump up and land with your feet a little more than shoulder width apart as you clap your hands over your head. I don't do my jumping jacks with weights. For me, jumping jacks increase cardiovascular function and act as a weight-bearing exercise to help protect against osteoporosis.

Walking/Cardio Routine

(20 to 30 minutes)

After my weight routine, I jump on my elliptical trainer and do at least twenty minutes of brisk "walking." If you don't have access to a machine such as this, take a brisk walk outdoors in the fresh air with a friend, hike a trail, ride a bicycle, play a game of tennis or golf, or take in any other fun activity that raises your heart rate. On the weekends, I head straight down to the beach and do my walking there.

To make my workout more enjoyable, I have a selection of great music on my iPod—favorite tunes with lively beats that I really love and look forward to listening and moving to. I never allow myself to listen to them at any other time; I keep them as a special treat for my workouts. I can listen to them at home or while I'm out walking. Here's a sampling of some of my music:

- "Here You Come Again," Dolly Parton
- "When I'm 64," The Beatles
- "King of the Road," Roger Miller
- "Tie a Yellow Ribbon Round the Old Oak Tree," Tony Orlando and Dawn
- "Sweet Gypsy Rose," Tony Orlando and Dawn
- "Come Fly with Me," Frank Sinatra, Luis Miguel
- "How Long Has This Been Going On?" Carly Simon
- "Amor, Amor, Amor," Luis Miguel
- "You Made Me a Woman," Barbara Lewis
- "Bésame Mucho," Luis Miguel

As you can see, I particularly love the wonderful Latin songs by Luis Miguel. There's nothing like a Latin beat to get you moving and put a smile on your face.

If I don't feel like music, I usually have the television on a channel with something enjoyable and a mug of coffee within reach. In other words, I make my workout time so enjoyable that time flies by and I actually miss my ritual on the rare occasions that I have to forego it.

What sounds like a lot is actually accomplished in about forty-five minutes. Within a few weeks of starting this routine, the habit of doing it every day was formed and I began to see and feel results. I noticed that my biceps and triceps had better tone and shape. Seeing results within a few weeks is an important part of the formula for developing the habit. Eventually, craving these workouts kicks in and it's hard to look back to a time when they weren't a part of daily life. Every so often I'll add more repetitions with the weights, walk a bit longer, or shake things up in some other way to continue to challenge myself.

Habits once formed can be difficult to break, and exercise is one good habit to develop. Have you ever heard that if you do something every day for twenty-one days, it becomes a habit? I think it's true. To make my commitment even easier, every night before going to bed, Wally pulls out the elliptical machine and sets it up in the den in front of the television so it will be waiting for me the next morning. Waking up and knowing it is there waiting for me like a friend is motivation enough. The fact that Wally takes it out each evening and puts it away each morning gives it more meaning than having it sitting there constantly as though it's another piece of furniture. If he has gone to the trouble of setting it up, the least I can do is use it.

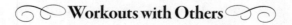

Workouts with Others

Because exercise comes in so many forms and has so many venues, it often isn't merely about keeping weight down or putting muscle on; it provides many emotional, mental, and social advantages. Whether you take part in golf, tennis, yoga, swimming, softball, or any other sport, you'll likely meet some wonderful people and develop solid friendships through related events and activities. For example, many golf tournaments or marathons entail volunteerism and philanthropy. The sense of community engendered by these events is remarkable and beneficial to everyone involved.

If there's one strong theme that has developed in our society, it's the acceptance that no matter what stage or age you're at, when you begin a workout routine or take up a sport, it's always accepted and encouraged by others who are already doing it. Options such as hiring a personal trainer for a one-on-one introduction to a routine or joining a beginners' running group or yoga class can satisfy your comfort level when you're getting started.

As I said earlier, my own routine is doable for me because I enjoy the convenience of exercising at home; it fits into my day perfectly. But you may be one of the many people who are motivated by going to the gym or taking a class. A membership at a gym or your local senior center can offer an abundance of opportunities besides treadmills and elliptical trainers. There is often a variety of classes available ranging from beginning to advanced levels. When looking into these classes, note that there are usually different instructors for each class and it's worth trying a few of them if your schedule permits. Finding the right instructor can make a big difference to how much you enjoy the class. Bring a full water bottle and wear appropriate clothing. One of the biggest advantages of establishing a routine of going to a class is meeting and bonding with the other regulars over sweat. Many friendships have been formed within gym walls, and believe me, they will notice if you miss a class.

Pilates and Yoga

Pilates and yoga classes are two choices that have you sitting, stretching, and performing moves and stances you would never normally think of doing. These classes are invigorating, and you'd be hard-pressed to find a more suitable workout to help a body age gracefully. Just be prepared to laugh at yourself if you're a beginner. Everyone goes through that awkward stage of figuring out the names of positions, let alone how to actually do them. It's a plight that is overcome with time if you stick with it, and the benefits are many. The low impact factor is great for seniors and those who can't endure high-impact exercises for health reasons. The slow, controlled movements help build a strong mental connection to each position and the transition between positions, so you feel the workout in your body, mind, and even soul. The poses will also keep your muscles long, supple, and graceful.

The primary concept with Pilates, yoga, and similar exercise methodologies is the coordination of breath and movement. Not only do these classes help you keep your circulatory and other systems healthy, but yoga in particular focuses on breathing. Although Joseph Pilates worked a great deal with returning war veterans, his ideas evolved and became popular with dancers, especially in New York City. His students became the teachers who have carried the Pilates tradition forward and helped develop its current fame. Joseph Pilates designed many exercises to bring the body into balance, as well as to lengthen and strengthen muscles.

Not only does having an instructor of some sort to guide you through your practice make it safer, but most likely there are others in the class from whom you can learn. A good certified instructor will make the class enjoyable, and hopefully you'll go back time and time again. One such instructor is Olava Menczkowska, who strives to provide a healthy, warm, safe environment for her clients. As an experienced Pilates and dance instructor, she encourages fluid and graceful movements in her classes.

Olava has been in the movement field for more than thirty years and has naturally seen changes in the workouts, the clients, and the age groups involved in her programs. "The paradigm of exercise has shifted, and I certainly see that in my own experience over the past ten, twenty, and thirty years," she explains. "The next wave, or the wave we seem to be in now, is where we're formulating a composite of those very same principles of breath and movement blended with other movement and dance forms to strike a chord of health, well-being, and physical functionality for today's more physically inactive world."

In reflecting on her clients, Olava says, "I have a lot of elderly people whom I absolutely adore. The ages range from ten to ninety years old in my classes." These are clients who return week after week, support one another, and bond as a community over stretching and feeling revitalized—literally to their core.

The ultimate goal for everyone taking a class in Pilates or yoga is to find their body's balance. Olava tells her clients, "Find your own music. Find your own breath. Find those, and there is the correlation between breath and music."

The benefits of all this stretching, posturing, and breathing properly are both visible and invisible. On the outside, you'll begin to see definition and tone you didn't have before. Your face will glow as you head out the door. But the benefits to your inner body are paramount. All of your systems—from

your circulatory system to your nervous system to systems you
don't even know about—can benefit from the alignment techniques of yoga and Pilates.

In some sense, these practices "unbunch" you. A workout
will leave you feeling fresh and untangled. In no time, you'll
find yourself sitting up straighter and walking taller due to
longer, toned muscles. The beauty of workouts such as these
is that they work in tandem with other sports or activities
you may be involved in. If it's the only exercise you do, that's
great, but if you cross train, you'll soon notice a positive difference in your other endeavors. The stretching and breathing give you a fluidity that lets you function much better in
everything you do.

If a class seems intimidating but you like the idea, try a
yoga or Pilates DVD. There are several options available. Mas-
ters such as Rodney Yee usually have several good yoga DVDs
especially for beginners. One is Peggy Cappy's *Yoga: For the
Rest of Us and More*.

Spinning and Aerobics

For a higher energy workout, spinning (indoor cycling) is a
favorite for many gym-goers. The low impact makes it fairly
easy on your body, but make sure to check your bike's settings
with an instructor before starting. The great thing about spinning is that while the instructor provides guidance throughout the class, you can go at your own pace to an extent. Not
only does it work your legs and raise your heart rate, but some
instructors incorporate upper-body movements such as little
push-ups into the routine. The upbeat music will keep you
going, and you should be prepared to sweat. Even beginning
classes will give you a hard workout.

Besides working with their own personal training clients, my daughter Darcy and her friend Suzanne Timerman also teach spinning at a few different gyms in Connecticut. As instructors, they highly recommend that their clients wear cycling shorts (padded for comfort) and, as with any aerobic class, bring a water bottle.

Consider introducing weights into your aerobic workout. There are classes (sometimes called "Body Pump") that incorporate weights with aerobics. Classes are guided by an instructor and the amount of weight you use depends on your desire and ability. It is advisable to wear comfortable clothes, especially those that wick sweat away from your body. The high energy of this workout allows you to tone muscles and burn fat all in one class. Now that's a great combination!

No matter what type of class you take, I recommend talking to the instructors beforehand to find out as much as you can about what to expect. A personal trainer may be able to give you some guidance as well. In general, classes run forty-five minutes to an hour or more, and if applicable, the gym will note which are beginner and advanced classes, so check the schedule.

Weight Training

If you want to expand your workout horizons and venture into weight training, I strongly urge you to sign up with a knowledgeable, certified, and experienced personal trainer. People take up weight training for a variety of reasons. Some want to add or tone muscles, while others know that muscle burns calories (fat doesn't). One of the best reasons for integrating weight training into your routine—one that Darcy and other trainers emphasize—is that the pure physical strength that comes from this training brings benefits to everyday situations. For example, the common tasks of carrying in the groceries, lifting your grandchild, or lugging a load of laundry downstairs all require a certain level of strength. Not convinced yet? Not only do toned muscles look leaner, but they are leaner. Think of it this way—fifteen pounds of muscle versus fifteen pounds of fat can mean the difference between wearing a size six or a size eight.

If you belong to a gym, make an appointment with a professional trainer to get you started. Weight training is one of those activities that requires guidance and knowledge of proper form in order to do it safely and gain the best results. John Cecalupo is a personal trainer in Charlottesville, Virginia, who works with several clients from the baby boomer generation. The three components of the workouts he designs are strength, joint stability, and flexibility. "After thirty, we lose 10 percent of our strength per decade if we're not working out," says Cecalupo. "Joint stability is critical, especially for shoulders, knees, and hips, because without that stability, the muscles can't function as well. People have the tendency to warm up their body temperature with a few minutes of aerobic activity, but they ought to add movement that promotes warming up the joints. If you take care of your joints, the muscles will follow."

Strengthening your core muscles is a necessity for building a strong body. According to Cecalupo, "It's not about having six-pack abs like everyone thinks. But if your core is strong and stable, the rest of your body can function from a strong base."

What surprises most of his clients is the concept that he prefers to start off with resistance training (incorporating weights) to build strength instead of focusing solely on aerobics such as the treadmill or elliptical trainer. "During the first twenty minutes of aerobics the body burns sugars, which is fine, but it takes at least thirty minutes of aerobic activity before it starts to burn fat. I integrate resistance training so that they build the strength they'll need to endure long periods of aerobics later."

Cecalupo's workouts are geared toward reducing the risk of osteoporosis through weight-bearing exercises: "With osteoporosis, the bones start to splinter, creating spaces in them. Using weight-bearing exercises, there's a compaction effect on the bones that counteracts osteoporosis. These exercises tie into developing the core strength needed to create balance in these workouts." Many of his clients use foam-coated bars rather than individual dumbbells, which when done properly, balances both sides of the body while lifting, creating the similar core strength that yoga or Pilates does.

My youngest daughter, Katy, sculpted her body with weights for several years in the late eighties and early nineties. Her natural athleticism landed her a spot as a contestant in the fourth season of "American Gladiators." She endured through to the grand championships, and much of her success was due not only to her strength, but to her agility and mental focus.

The Great Outdoors

The activities described so far in this chapter have been geared toward indoor workouts. For outdoor enthusiasts, traditional activities such as golf, tennis, running, cycling, hiking, kayaking, skiing, and others vary in intensity, price of participation, degree of difficulty, and availability. My daughters Darcy, Anne, and Heather are all cyclists who engage in the sport for different reasons. Darcy competes, Heather uses it as a muse for her writing, and Anne enjoys casual mountain biking with friends. They all have their own motivations, yet they all benefit from the same activity.

Sports like swimming can naturally be done inside or out, depending on the season. Gyms with swimming pools often have water aerobic classes available, and local colleges and city centers may open both indoor and outdoor pools to the community. There are websites such as meetup.com that can help you locate other outdoor sporting enthusiasts. This is especially helpful if you're new to both the sport and an area and want to meet people while exercising outdoors.

❧ What Works for You ❧

The beautiful thing about exercise is that it doesn't have to be routine or forced. The options are endless in so many ways: availability, simplicity, cost of equipment or fees, team or group activities versus individual workouts—the list goes on and on, as does the list of benefits. If you can find your niche in the workout world, you'll be certain to open new doors to a physically healthier and happier future.

What entices you to jump out of bed in the morning? The aroma of coffee brewing in your kitchen? Or is it the thought of going to the gym or out for a walk or run? When exercise influences your ability to get up early in the morning, you know you're living a vital life. You know you'll feel alive and vibrant by the time you finish running, lifting weights, swimming, or stretching. If you've never caught the exercise bug, know that it can be contagious at any age. In fact, I've heard of many people who start jogging or running in their sixties and seventies. These inspirational individuals are highly regarded for their willingness to begin new endeavors, especially challenging ones. Many of them enter races and bask in how much younger they feel coming down the home stretch with people half their age. Even if they walk over the finish line, their accomplishment is a worthy one, and their stories are written up in the papers as lifestyle or sports stories. No matter where you see these newfound athletes, note the large smiles on their faces. Those smiles are there because they feel alive and have discovered one of the secrets to capturing youth. Their doctors often report that they have reduced cholesterol and lower blood pressure. Family members comment on their good moods. Years drop off their faces, and just being around them leaves you feeling invigorated. It is contagious. Go to any track early in the morning, and I bet you'll see some newly indoctrinated walkers alongside joggers who have some years behind them. I clink my water bottle to theirs.

The ideal way to begin any program is to start with small, achievable goals and build up to a full routine. The best of intentions, as you'll know from your own New Year's resolutions, fail when you take on more than you can handle at one time. Examine your daily and weekly schedule and plug in planned time for exercise. Fix that time on your calendar the same way you would a doctor's appointment, business meeting, or an event with friends or family. If you can't make a trip to the gym to spend an hour on the treadmill, plan a long, brisk walk as you go about your day. Make your time work efficiently, and be realistic about how you're going to make exercise an ongoing part of your life. Two fifteen-minute workouts or three ten-minute workouts spread throughout the day are beneficial as well. Fit in what you can—it might be that some days you can do a full thirty minutes and others you will have to break up your exercise. Be flexible and it will work.

My children's experiences have been much different than my own. They are all athletic and have been involved in sports since they were young. With six of them, they could always play in teams, involving many of the other kids where we lived. They grew up playing basketball, softball, football, track, field hockey, baseball, ice hockey, and other team sports, as well as participating in cycling and figure skating. During the summers they swam and played pool games. I, on the other hand, was famous in my family for doing "vertical laps" in the pool— basically bobbing up and down. Since I grew up skating on the ice rink at Rockefeller Center in New York, it was fun to watch my children when they took up the same activity at the Greenwich Skating Club. Figure skating and ice hockey were imbedded into our winters for many years, and I loved getting out there on the ice with them. To this day, they are all active. In addition to my daughters' sports, described previously, my eldest son, Jim, plays softball on a "media" league for NBC in Charlotte, North Carolina, and weight trains. Gus, who produces "Baseball Tonight," plays on an ESPN recreational team. It's not surprising that they are still involved with sports, since it was engrained in them when they were young. It's interesting that they have all found what works best for them and don't think twice about doing whatever it is they do.

I would like to end this chapter with a great quote by Gloria Steinem. Apparently someone remarked to her that she didn't look fifty, to which Steinem answered, "My dear, this is what fifty looks like." Finding a healthy and safe way to mesh exercise into your schedule allows you to enjoy your body well into old age. Whether with friends, in a class, or on your own, it's an essential aspect to aging gracefully.

Chapter 4

The Benefits of Proper Nutrition and Sleep

A good laugh and a long sleep are the best cures in the doctor's book.

—*Irish Proverb*

"What am I going to eat?" Whether staring at the inside of your refrigerator or at a menu in a restaurant, this question hounds us. Yet many of us fall into the trap of eating the same foods the majority of the time—almost the way we wear 10 percent of our wardrobe 90 percent of the time. The problem is that once we develop eating habits, not only is it hard to change them, but we often don't realize we've created the habits in the first place. Even if we're choosing to eat healthy foods, if the menu isn't varied, it's unlikely that we're giving ourselves the nutritionally balanced diet needed to maintain optimum health, energy, and well-being.

I learned to accept and embrace the notion that nutrition weighs in as one of the most important aspects of maintaining health and youthfulness. In 2003 when my modeling career was unfolding, I consulted Derek Johnson, a renowned nutrition expert and dietician and the founder of New Metabolism. I not only wanted to ensure my future health, but I also wanted to increase my energy level. Both of these were essential to keeping up with the demands of my position as public relations manager at a world-renowned golf resort and an increasing number of modeling assignments. Johnson's proven outlook and philosophies on nutrition, along with the personal program he designed for me, provided the balance I needed to juggle my hectic schedule and the many meals I eat away from home.

What You Really Put in Your Mouth

Even if you believe you eat a healthy diet, working with an established nutritionist will open your eyes to so much more than what you put in your mouth. As a foundation for all of his clients' programs, Johnson uses a nutritional analysis that includes personal and family histories, a physical activity profile, a dietary assessment, segmental body fat testing, and a blood test. While much of the dietary advice Johnson provides is universal, all of his clients have their own body chemistry makeup, which he looks at when determining what's missing from their diets. A personalized program based on the results of his analysis leads to an optimum eating plan for each person's body and lifestyle.

I was impressed with this approach because it focuses on two vital areas that unhealthy people often neglect—proper digestion and sleep requirements. Working toward proper digestion made sense to me, but I wouldn't have thought that sleep mattered as much as it does when it comes to nutrition. For these reasons and many more, Johnson opposes fad diets that produce short-term, unsustainable results, especially because these diets go against the two core requirements of adequate digestion and sleep. What I love about his approach is that he looks at the body image as a whole, as well as how his clients feel about themselves emotionally and physically.

New Metabolism's "Ten Simple Rules" (see sidebar) are a great place for anyone to start. This list is taped to my bathroom mirror as a reminder of the simple daily steps I can take toward being healthier. These steps have now become habits, just like brushing my teeth. While not complicated, the plan that Johnson devises for me changes as my schedule and routine change, such as when I'm traveling or have a modeling assignment on the horizon. For instance, he suggested that I eat more protein and fewer carbs for a few days before a modeling assignment so I don't get the bloated-belly feeling that can kick in by four o'clock. I've also found that the well-known mantra of a big, healthy breakfast, a balanced lunch, and a light dinner early in the evening works wonders for keeping my tummy flat and knocking off a couple of pounds for that all-important occasion.

My positive approach to life meshed well with Johnson's conviction that you have to become healthy to lose weight. In my case, it was a matter of building muscle tissue, which can add weight to an already slight frame. So, although weight loss wasn't an issue for me, finding energy through my diet and adding muscle tone were critical. There are several body types, and being thin doesn't necessarily mean you're healthier than someone who needs to shed some weight. Also, you need to redefine *weight* as "body fat" rather than the number you read on the scale. Muscle tissue and body fat are what matter, and most women do not have enough muscle. It's about your clothing size, not the number on the scale. In regards to the philosophy of being healthy to lose weight, Johnson adds, "You have

New Metabolism's Ten Simple Rules to Strive for

1. Drink a glass of water first thing every morning.

2. Eat slowly and sit down at every meal.

3. Eat breakfast or a snack within forty-five minutes of waking.

4. Try never to eat a carbohydrate by itself; add a fat or protein.

5. Never go longer than four hours without eating.

6. Drink at least sixty-four ounces of water daily (small amounts at meals).

7. Eat dinner by seven o'clock.

8. Take at least one fifteen-minute break outside the office each day.

9. Make sure to get eight hours of uninterrupted sleep.

10. Choose natural carbohydrates—the ones that come from the ground—such as rice, yams, sweet potatoes, and beans.

to be healthy for the body to maintain its ideal weight; you cannot force it to do so from dieting."

The skinny is that many underweight people are starved for crucial nutrients, meaning they are technically unhealthy. "In actuality, many thin people feel much worse than overweight people, but you would never know it from their looks," he explains. "The body is malnourished, which means it starts to use muscle for energy. This is what puts women at more risk for osteopenia, the precursor of osteoporosis. Each person's body knows exactly where its healthy weight is, and it's our job to fuel the body properly so that it can do the rest. By eating the right foods and fueling the body each day, it will build and maintain the right amount of muscle and keep off any unwanted body fat."

Like exercise, a sensible, balanced diet should become a habit, which is why fad programs don't work. Any limited diet may take weight off initially, but those diets are not healthy in the long run and are impossible to stick to—they are technically designed to fail. It has been proven over and over that you need a balance of protein, carbohydrates, and fats. So go for the long haul. While you may lose weight at a slower pace, it will stay off and you'll feel much better.

Need more reasons to eat well? How about antiaging? What usually comes to mind when you think of looking younger? Probably hair color, shampoos, skin care formulas and creams, or supplements. Johnson notes, "Trying to just look healthy on the outside isn't as important as becoming healthy on the inside. The answer once again is proper sleep and digestion. You cannot trick the body long term; that only works with short-term things like makeup and eye creams. But we have to remember to treat the cause, not the symptom. For example, someone may have a stomachache, bloating, or gas several times a week, so we commonly identify things like food allergies from simple blood tests that might be the cause of these symptoms. Remember, if you're not healthy from the beginning, your body isn't going to maintain the results you desire. This goes for all types of people, from stay-at-home moms to professional athletes."

Digestion, Johnson admits, is not a "cool" thing to talk about, but even if you're eating well and taking supplements, if you're not taking in the right nutrients, your daily function is thrown off. "There's a laundry list of things your body must have to stay alive—pretty skin and nails are at the bottom of the list. In terms of antiaging, the body's largest organ is the skin, and it tells everything about us—it comes back to digesting and absorbing foods properly."

When I first met with Johnson, he asked me two basic questions: what foods I liked and how I felt throughout the day. He said, "Get your body in tune as much as you can through food, because without that, it's an uphill battle." These words still resonate with me.

With the kids grown and gone, baby boomers finally have the chance to take care of themselves. It's never too late to start focusing on your health, even if you haven't done so yet. Diets in the United States tend to be acidic, and acidic bodies are a sickness magnet. We all know about heart disease and diabetes. "You pay for things later in life because the body has a funny way of letting you know eventually that you didn't take care of it. The better the body functions, the better it's going to recover and repair," Johnson reminds his clients. "Your body is constantly changing. It adapts to both good and bad environments alike. Yet it doesn't always tell you you're being unhealthy, which is why heart disease is the number-one killer in women. A few of the fundamental rules about nutrition are fact. It's unfortunate that people take the basic concepts of nutrition and try and make up their own rules. . . . Over time, everything we eat has a direct effect on our health, and that's a fundamental fact that can't be manipulated."

As I discussed in Chapter 3, I didn't incorporate a regular workout routine into my schedule until later in life. Incidentally, this is one of Johnson's requirements—that each client create a workout routine that integrates resistance training. "To build muscle tone, it's important to do resistance training, especially for clients who aren't that mobile and can't move around due to a bad hip," he notes. "There are exercises they can do if they're shown how to do them properly."

Johnson discusses osteoporosis with clients as young as their thirties and forties and with thinner clients because they often aren't getting the proper nutritional absorption that comes from a lack of muscle tissue. He loves the idea of getting in a swimming pool with floaties for resistance training, saying that it's "often better than any medicine they can take."

Winning the antiaging war doesn't happen overnight, but it is truly amazing what the body can do and recover from once you come face-to-face with what food is and how it works inside your body. When you're eating foods that work well for you, you don't have to worry about digesting. Coupled with a good night's sleep, that can take years off your looks and add them to your life.

Valerie's Nutritional Program

I've always had a sweet tooth, and my personal nutritional program revolves around curbing my cookie cravings. Since the brain runs on glucose, you create an imbalance when you eat a lot of sugar; the brain tries to catch up and you end up in a constant flux of too much sugar or not enough. Derek taught me that by increasing the protein and "good" carbohydrates in my diet and having fruit for a snack, I could decrease my cookie cravings. It was difficult at first, but I soon found out that he was right. The discovery of a cracker (carried by Whole Foods) that is both gluten-free and low in sugar really helped. You can spread a thin layer of almond or peanut butter on a few of these crackers and feel just as satisfied as you would have if you'd eaten an oatmeal raisin cookie! Check your health food store or grocery store for cookies that don't contain any of the "bad" ingredients you want to avoid and that are still tasty—just as good as their more fattening counterparts. When I want to treat myself to a cookie, I'll reach for one or two of these.

One item Johnson removed from my diet was soy protein powder, substituting whey protein powder instead. He explained to me that soy is not a desirable form of protein for many reasons, one being that it does not contain all of the essential amino acids. "Soy is fine if it's an old-fashioned fermented soy product such as miso, tempeh, and natto, all of which can be incorporated into any type of lifestyle. Using soy milk, soy protein powder, and soy burgers—things we've marketed and used misleading and false information about in the United States—can reduce the assimilation of iron," he notes. "Remember, the United States is one of the unhealthiest nations in the world. And one of the most overweight, too. There is solid evidence linking soy to malnutrition, digestive problems, thyroid dysfunction, cognitive decline, reproductive disorders, immune system breakdowns, even heart disease and cancer. Whey protein is so much better. It's great for smoothies and is perfect for a postworkout drink. Make sure to add glutamine to the protein shake, which is important for the lining of the stomach and helps build mass for muscle tissue." My personal favorite is to whip up a shake of protein powder, orange-flavored Emergen-C, two ounces of orange juice, and six ounces of light cran-raspberry juice or water. For a meal on the run, I'll pop this in a thermos, grab a protein bar, and I head out the door.

Together, Johnson and I added several foods to my diet, including whole eggs, more vegetables, fish, tuna, fruits (berries are best), peanut and almond butter, kidney and black beans, chicken, turkey, rice crackers, hummus, salads, pita or gluten-free cinnamon raisin bread (just because I love anything cinnamon raisin, and it's a better choice than cookies), real fruit jams, and goat cheese. Integrating Johnson's plan with my workouts has helped me build muscle, retain energy, and get the stamina and kick I need for a long day of modeling shoots or runway shows.

Nutrition and eating right needn't be daunting. There are ample resources available in magazines, books, and television shows in addition to doctors and professional nutritionists. The trick is learning how to weed through the data to find the nuggets you need. Keep away from fads and trendy diets because they often result in more damage than benefit. Prepare your grocery list at home by looking through your refrigerator and pantry—are there enough fruits, vegetables, and grains? Glance through a yummy, nutritious cookbook for appealing recipes and jot down the needed ingredients. Many cookbooks these days provide nutritional data—something they didn't do when I was a young mother. If you can help it, never go to the grocery store when you're hungry, which makes impulse buying irresistible. Prepare your list and then stick to it.

Old habits are easier to break when they're replaced with a new, desirable habit. What do you have to lose? A few pounds? And what you'll gain will reward you tenfold.

You Are What You Sleep

There are many evenings when I entertain travel writers, celebrities, or producers at one of the many famous restaurants on the Monterey Peninsula. Besides the challenge of eating healthy while dining out, late dinners result in late nights and my sleep suffers as a result. The greatest taboo of all is having a big dinner topped off with a sugar-laden dessert and anything more than one glass of wine. As for after-dinner drinks? Unless you're a total glutton for punishment, forget about them. The sugar in alcohol on top of a dessert is a surefire way to go home, climb into bed, sleep for a couple of hours, and then find yourself maddeningly awake for the rest of the night. I might add that the next day isn't much fun either.

Of course, I'm not the only one with a hectic schedule. New Metabolism's diverse client list includes athletes, celebrities, professionals, and stay-at-home moms, and all of these people benefit in their own way from Derek Johnson's consultations. As your life evolves, your nutritional needs warrant different solutions. It seems like a lifetime ago that I was a young mother who only caught a few hours of sleep a night.

"New moms in particular rarely achieve the required amount of consistent sleep," Johnson says. "Sleep is required if you don't want to age, because you have to repair the damage done to your body during the day. If you want to repair properly, it's important that you get the proper amount of sleep. Most women are deprived of sleep because they take care of everyone but themselves." During the first ten years of motherhood, I didn't get much sleep—very little, in fact. My first five children were born between fourteen and seventeen months apart. After I gave birth to Darcy, my second, I sometimes slept as little as two hours a night, and it was broken sleep at that because she suffered from terrible colic. When Gus, my fifth, came along, we endured a three-month period starting when he was six weeks old when all five of them came down with chicken pox two weeks apart. It seemed to go on forever and resulted in many nights of lost sleep as we dealt with the itchy rashes. It gives me the shudders just remembering it. That was the kind of thing you have to be young to survive; it would be much more difficult for an older mom to handle.

Nowadays my life is filled with a different kind of adrenaline, and sleep can still be a challenge. From the excitement of landing my first modeling assignment to finding out I was going to appear on the "Today Show," the adrenaline still kicks in, but it doesn't act as a supplement to healthy eating.

The ideal is eight hours of uninterrupted sleep, according to Johnson, who supports the results of studies that recommend this number; however, the key is to obtain at least six hours of uninterrupted sleep. Each person's body requires varying amounts within those guidelines. A lot of people don't realize what's happening to their bodies when they wake up in the middle of the night to use the bathroom or get a drink of water. As Johnson explains, "Our bodies are a chemistry lab, not a bank account. When we interrupt sleep patterns, the process of healing the damage done from the previous day is self-defeating. We add to the damage by losing sleep, and we lose out on critical healing that comes from reaching the levels of sleep cycles."

Working, grocery shopping, working out, and chasing kids around take a toll on your body. Adequate sleep habits repair the damage. "Working on getting solid sleep first is important, and it's never too late to start getting quality sleep," states Johnson. "Staying asleep to get through the sleep cycles, creating that consistency, means you don't want to wake up and restart during the night, or in the morning you'll wake up groggy. Sleep is where we repair from a day's activity. Exercise and activity put us in the red, and the more we stay in the deficit, the more damage we cause. Injuries are more likely to occur then."

Quality sleep and proper nutrition are the foundation for healthy aging. The combination of the two gives us the fuel needed to balance everything else in our lives and assists in preventing disease of the body, mind, and soul.

Chapter 5

Healthy Aging

O f all the self-fulfilling prophecies in our culture, the assumption that aging means decline and poor health is probably the deadliest.

—*Marilyn Ferguson,* The Aquarian Conspiracy

Naturally I wanted to devote a chapter to the medical side of combating ageism. After all, we are starting to face (or are already facing) health issues we didn't worry about when we were young and carefree. The years of using our bodies catch up to us eventually, but fortunately there is more information than ever available about choices related to health and wellness. Part of my approach to aging gracefully certainly entails taking care of my physical well-being. Whether it's making sure I go for all of my annual exams or using alternative approaches to fend off illness or disease, my health is always at the forefront of my mind—in a good way.

Luckily for me, I have built a relationship with two physicians, Arlene and Rick Noodleman; I was asked to model for their cosmetic dermatology and healthy aging medical center, Age Defy Dermatology and Wellness, located in California's Silicon Valley. What started as a modeling job evolved into a special opportunity to share our mutual passion for healthy aging and wellness.

This chapter encapsulates both my own message and a medical perspective on healthy and graceful aging. Arlene Noodleman, M.D., M.P.H., is a board-certified preventive medicine physician; her approach to patient care bridges both Eastern and Western philosophies of health and combats "*dis*-ease," a term for when our well-being is challenged by illness. Her integrative model encompasses promoting wellness of the body, mind, and soul while embracing advanced medical techniques to slow the onset of the aging process. The Noodlemans' Look Well and Live Well services are rooted in Western medicine and time-honored healing traditions that include modern preventive and screening approaches, nutritional counseling, movement therapy, exercise prescriptions, acupuncture, mindfulness-based stress reduction, and energy-based treatments such as therapeutic massage and Healing Touch. Through these methods, patients achieve a balanced, healthier life, which are the keys to healthy, successful aging.

While Arlene Noodleman is the first to agree that aging is inevitable, the development of age-related disease is not. We *can* age gracefully by choosing behaviors that promote health. The goal is to use a flexible, balanced approach that leaves us feeling younger for as long as possible.

These ideas remind me of a quote by Karl von Bonstetten: "To resist old age, one must combine the body, the mind, and the heart—and to keep them in parallel vigor, one must exercise, study, and love." Some baby boomers are doing just that, as evidenced by the second careers they are embarking on and the dreams they continue to follow. Maintaining a youthful spirit is especially important in slowing the aging process. No matter how well we take care of our bodies and minds, if we are spiritually depleted, we will not age well. Invigorate your spirit by keeping your body and mind balanced through practicing wellness.

The Quest for Wellness

In a chapter on healthy aging, you might expect to see separate sections on heart disease, osteoporosis, arthritis, cancer, and so on, but that's just the kind of thinking that Dr. Noodleman and I are trying to get away from. Instead, we embrace the idea of focusing on wellness. *Wellness*, as defined by the National Wellness Association, is "an active process of becoming aware of and making choices toward a more successful existence." The health benefits of addressing the combined role of the body, mind, and soul in achieving and maintaining balance in our health and lifestyle is of more interest to people now than ever before. Whether in the checkout line at a health food store or on the magazine racks at a bookstore, you'll find a wide variety of publications that focus on the many aspects of wellness. The respect and demand for such information has increased enormously since veggie burgers hit the mainstream marketplace several years ago.

The idea of wellness is strongly based in Eastern philosophies rather than Western-based medicine. As you will see, there are many Eastern-based preventive measures you can take advantage of to reduce your odds of ending up in a doctor's office (other than for your routine exams). Along with the physical and nutritional information I gave you in the Chapters 3 and 4, Dr. Noodleman's expansive knowledge rounds out the concept of wellness at any age. We now have many more choices and options to turn to than we did during our teenage years.

Dr. Noodleman points out that Eastern philosophy encourages a long, healthy, vibrant life up until the very end. But in our current Western tradition, we often do not enjoy good health in our later years. Instead, many suffer from lifestyle- and age-related chronic diseases, such as diabetes, heart disease, and cancer that take the joy out of life. Western medicine's disease-based model focuses on a "reductionistic" approach with highly mechanistic, technical paradigms that reduce our bodies to isolated parts, such as individual organs and biochemical pathways. When one of these parts needs medical attention, it can be targeted by certain drugs, surgery, and/or other medical interventions.

The idea is to avoid the need for these interventions. Two encouraging Western alternatives to medical reductionism are the specialties of preventive and integrative medicine, disciplines that take into consideration the whole person, rather than just individual parts. Prevention and intervention strategies combat disease before the physical manifestations of it have occurred in order to discover the real source of the problem. Often the culprit is an unhealthy lifestyle or behavior.

Luckily it's never too late to change; both Western and Eastern traditions can inspire us to make changes to promote health, prevent disease, and live well longer. While many people know what they *should* be doing (that is, eating right, exercising, and reducing stress), few know how to make the necessary behavioral changes that they can maintain for any significant length of time. For example, although people may lose a substantial amount of weight through dieting, the majority of them gain the weight right back. This can lead to a

vicious cycle of diet and weight gain, which has its own associated health problems. Programs such as Age Defy's Healthy
Lifestyle are designed to break this cycle and are based on the
principles of integrative and behavioral medicine. Each program emphasizes the importance of gradual lifestyle change
in adopting healthier behaviors until eventually an improved
lifestyle can be sustained.

The Problem of Stress

Combating stress is one of the first things we think of when we
talk about achieving wellness in our lives. Stress is an imbalance
in our lives that leaves us in varying degrees of disruption. It is
caused by both short-term situations, such as a public speaking engagement, rush-hour traffic, and flying on an airplane,
and life-altering stressors like divorce, the death of a loved one,
and job loss. There are times when stress seems inescapable and
maybe it is, but we often put more stress on our minds and
bodies than we need to by worrying about things that may not
(and usually don't) ever happen. Figuring out how we react
to different types of stressful situations is a great first step in
reducing our overall stress level. Negative thought patterns
often go hand-in-hand with stress, leaving us unhealthy in our
bodies, minds, and, especially, our souls.

Our spirits become depleted through lifelong, negative
thought patterns and a loss of vitality in all areas of life; in
other words, they succumb to internalized ageism. It's important to correct these patterns, which can be done by learning
about the different methods available to increase energy and
reduce stress. One effective way is through a mindfulness-

based stress reduction (MBSR) program. First developed by Jon Kabat Zinn and based on the ancient Buddhist practice of mindfulness, MBSR helps students take an active role in managing their health, teaching them to become more aware of their thoughts and feelings and to change their relationship to those thoughts and feelings. These programs have been used not only for personal meditation, but in more than two hundred hospitals around the world. It's a remarkably effective way to improve not only our thoughts and emotions, but also our overall physical health.

It's universally understood that stress impacts us physically, mentally, and emotionally. Because it works from the inside out, it takes a toll on our physical "envelope"—the skin, meaning stress can literally be written all over our faces. At Age Defy, they call this the "complexion connection." Making changes to reduce stress and promote a sense of well-being may also decrease the effects of stress on the skin, improving conditions such as acne, rosacea, and even eczema. Plus, we just look more relaxed.

Healthy Aging and Your Skin

Healthy aging—not antiaging—is the most appropriate and encouraging way to look at turning back the clock when it comes to keeping our skin looking young and bright. It's not about masking age; it's about maintaining age-appropriate skin as we get older. The focus should always be on following a plan to achieve healthier skin. A natural by-product is that as the skin becomes healthier, it also looks better. It becomes radiant, smoother, and more evenly toned.

Arlene Noodleman says that both Eastern and Western approaches can address the outward signs of aging. They are largely due to oxidative stress and the subsequent production of destructive free radicals, which result in the "three Ds": deflation, deterioration, and descent. In the West, cosmetic surgery is commonly used to combat the three Ds. However, "extreme makeovers" may result in an unnatural, expressionless look. Some women are so overdone that they actually have an almost "pickled" appearance. Our youth-obsessed society has lost sight of the essential components of aging gracefully: balance and moderation. Outward appearance is overemphasized, while the most important characteristics of youth—energy, resilience, flexibility, balance, and strength—are often overlooked.

When Science Helps to Defy Aging

There are countless products, treatments, and procedures out there for defying aging, and the use of them is a personal decision to be made with input from a reputable physician. I've used Botox in the furrow between my eyes a few times but would not use it anywhere else, although I know people who have with good results. The key with any procedure or treatment—and I can't stress this enough—is to go to a board-certified doctor with a great reputation. Do your research before allowing anyone to perform a treatment. There are plenty of excellent, highly qualified doctors out there. You can look at medical articles and journals; then ask around among your friends and colleagues. Check the credentials and specialties of your possible choices with the American Medical Association at ama-assn. org. Get as much information as you can. Be sure you choose a procedure that is suitable for you—one that is going to get the best results for what you want to achieve at a price and time commitment you can afford. Select a doctor for her abilities and safety rating rather than someone who may be famous for working with celebrities or having fancy offices and a huge practice. Your aim is to find competent care from someone you can relate to personally.

Another treatment I've received is photo rejuvenation. This treatment is performed with a cool-tip laser, meaning no downtime for healing. It reduces fine lines, wrinkles, sun damage, and rosacea; helps to tighten the skin; and aids in building collagen. It's not a dermabrasion or a peel. I used it to get rid of age spots and sun damage on my face.

My personal approach to aging gracefully does not include extremely invasive cosmetic surgery. Rather, I embrace the concepts Dr. Noodleman speaks about so passionately. I have chosen some wonderful, minimally invasive options, such as copper bromide laser treatments to diminish unwanted blood vessels and repair damage incurred by too many summers in the California sun as a teenager. I now enjoy a healthier looking complexion and a more even skin tone.

I've also tried and liked Botox. When performed by a board-certified dermatologist, the treatments are extremely safe and give me a rested, refreshed look. I especially like to smooth the furrow between my eyebrows—no point in having frown lines when they're so easy to get rid of! Another treatment I have experienced firsthand is Sculptra soft tissue correction. Unlike wrinkle "fillers," Sculptra is not a synthetic substance; it is a naturally derived "booster" made of poly-L-lactic acid that stimulates your body to produce its own collagen. Gradually, the treated areas fill out for a smoother, more youthful look. I have also used Sculptra to plump the loose skin on my hands with excellent results.

Top Ten Wellness Tidbits

1. According to the American Institute of Stress, up to 90 percent of all health problems are related to stress.

2. Research confirms that our thoughts and emotions have a dynamic effect on our health and vitality.

3. Acupuncture, MBSR, therapeutic massage, and energy-based treatments facilitate healing and complement cosmetic dermatology and rejuvenating medical/spa treatments. All of these methods activate the body's natural reparative processes, reduce stress, and help achieve a balanced, healthier life.

4. Scientific studies have found a strong link between the complexion and emotions. Activities designed to improve the emotional state have the added benefit of improving the quality of the skin, which in turn decreases stress and further improves the emotional state.

5. The immune system and the body's ability to heal quickly are directly affected by stress and overall mind-body health.

6. An anti-inflammatory diet, such as the traditional Japanese and Mediterranean diets, may promote health and decrease the chances of developing age-related diseases.

7. While baby boomers have aged in years, most haven't aged in spirit. Many are not retiring so they can spend their days at home. Instead, they're living active lifestyles, traveling, even trying second careers. For them, retirement represents an opportunity to live out their dreams.

8. Eastern philosophies and practices are readably available in the Western world as more people accept them with open hearts and minds.

9. The best approach to preventing, modifying, or even reversing the changes that time brings is not denying the aging process, but rather making behavior choices that help delay the onset of age-related decline and disease for as long as possible.

10. Beauty and wellness go hand in hand. Our skin-care regimen, fitness level, and lifestyle choices all affect how we look and feel.

ᔔ The Dangers of Inflammation ᔕ

Another factor that affects how we age is the role of prolonged inflammation in the development of many chronic, degenerative diseases. Inflammation has now been implicated in the development of coronary artery disease, atherosclerosis, Alzheimer's disease, autoimmune diseases, and even cancer. While the inflammatory process is essential to defending, maintaining, and repairing the body, uncontrolled, abnormal inflammation can be detrimental to long-term health. Arlene Noodleman stresses the critical role that inflammation plays in many diseases. For example, it's long been thought that deposits of cholesterol on the lining of the arteries are the root cause of heart disease. However, cholesterol plaques that critically narrow coronary arteries may actually be a reaction to chronic inflammation in the lining of these vessels. Likewise, a hallmark of Alzheimer's disease is the accumulation of amyloid, which scientists now believe develops as a result of inflammation in the brain.

While treating hardened arteries using Western-based treatments such as drugs, bypass surgery, or angioplasty is often beneficial, lasting lifestyle changes may be equally—and in some cases even more—effective. Such changes include stress reduction; moderate, regular exercise; and a diet rich in fresh fruits, vegetables, and anti-inflammatory omega-3 fats (found in foods such as salmon, flaxseed, and walnuts). Taken together, Eastern- and Western-based medicines offer a comprehensive approach to preventing disease and promoting healthy aging.

Aging gracefully in body, mind, and soul can have lasting, positive effects on our health. The Eastern and Western approaches discussed in this chapter can delay the onset of the aging process and prevent the constriction and deterioration of our bodies, minds, and spirits. These ideas underlie many of the concepts presented in this book. As evidenced in Chapters 3, 8, and 15, the philosophies are complementary and support my desire to help people by sharing knowledge about how to age gracefully with an audience thirsty for the information. This is, after all, what makes the journey worthwhile.

Chapter 6

The Seasoned Sensualities of Sexuality

L ife is not about how many breaths we take, but how many moments take our breath away.

—*Anonymous*

One of the many things that makes life so interesting is the unexpected surprises that come your way. It is having the experiences that you never in a million years thought you would have. Writing this chapter is certainly one of those for me, but it's also one that I've looked forward to because, let's face it, few subjects are more universal or of more interest to men and women alike than sexuality. As we grow older, it's an area that increasingly enriches our lives and makes the world a more beautiful place.

If ever there was a meeting ground for body, mind, and soul, the connection between two people in love is certainly it. So much of your sexuality resides in your mind, and when you love someone, it is not the physical being you fall in love with (although that may well be part of the initial attraction) but the essence of the person's soul. When your deepest feelings and emotions enter the equation, then your spirit soars and your heart really does take flight.

Sexuality in the later part of life is not as much about having great sex (although that can be a part of it) as it is about the core essentials of communication and intimacy. The combination of the two provides fuel that sparks the fire within you. Additionally—and I know some people would argue this point—I deeply believe that a healthy sex life and sensual attitude adds tremendous value to a relationship and your own well-being. There are ways of expressing sexuality later in life that are often uncharted in our youth—breaking down boundaries and exploring the benefits and importance of intimacy and communication established through touch, laughter (very important under any circumstance, but particularly as you get older), and the confidence to take risks and try new things. Sexual communication strengthens intimacy and enriches the bond between lovers, allowing for continuous growth in the relationship.

Any ongoing partnership requires work, and partners who care enough to make the effort to explore different ways of being together as they change (both physically and emotionally) will certainly reap the rewards. Partners who are able to adapt to a new style of sexuality as life progresses, rather than shutting down, maintain a certain level of both verbal and physical communication.

The Art of Keeping Sexuality Alive

I think we are so fortunate to be living in a time when sex is no longer considered taboo for women, especially seasoned ones. Historically, desire was something to be swept under the carpet and denied. Now, as medical advances help women live well and live longer, sexuality is recognized as a key element to the overall person. It is something to be celebrated as a rich and fulfilling part of the whole life experience. Not only is sexuality good for your health, but it enriches your life in many other ways. It keeps the sparkle in your eyes, the bounce in your step, and the radiance in your smile. Sexual expression wears many faces; that's one of the things that keeps it lively and interesting. Love has many moods. One encounter may be sweet and tender or comforting or it can be just plain lusty, while still another may take on a sense of daring or adventure.

With a smile and a willingness to take risks, try making love in a brand-new way in a brand-new place. It's hard to get bored if routine doesn't have the chance to set in. It's also easy to fall into a pattern of allowing your lover to be the aggressor, but men love it when women take them by surprise and switch roles on them. Your partner wants and needs to know that you have needs, too. It's a wonderful reminder for him that there are times when your desires well up just as strongly as his do. When you open up to him and tell him how you're feeling, it makes your bond that much stronger. Mutual appreciation, caring, and loving acts benefit both of you. Don't try things just for him; fulfill your own desires and needs. The idea is to keep the relationship fresh by being open to all of the different ways in which you can express your sexuality. Communicating sexually in a healthy, established relationship keeps the doors of communication open in other areas as well.

There is no doubt that there are days when exhaustion or distraction leaves you uninterested in anything more than a cold drink and your favorite chair. But once in a while, consider taking a moment to move outside yourself, to draw your partner into your world, using touch to unwind into a cozy communication. It won't take long, and you'll be amazed at how the fatigue drains away and the problems of the day are forgotten. Instead of giving in to the temptation of that easy chair, strip off your work clothes and head for the shower. Let the warm water beat down on your muscles as you feel fatigue disappear down the drain in a swirl of bubbles. Invite your partner to join you, and put on whatever music strikes your fancy. Slip into something lacy and fun, think about something sexually stimulating, pick up a steamy novel, or turn on a movie that gets your motor going. As arousal takes hold, you're like a runner about to start a race—focused and raring to go. Your heartbeat quickens and your breath comes a little faster. Shrugging off the doldrums of the day and allowing sensuality in creates an escape that can ease you into sleep with sweet dreams.

Candles and scented oils are easy to keep on hand and only take a moment to light. The added fragrance touches on a few of the five senses—candles not only fill the room with a sensual aroma, but the flickering flames and dancing shadows add a visual ambience. Massage oils, especially when used with care, emphasize touch and tenderness. Music engages hearing, while intimate kissing stimulates taste. Spin these together and not only do you have romance, but also relaxation and fulfilled desire. Use your imagination and enjoy!

Naturally, I'm not saying you have to do this every night, but if you're married or in a relationship, it should certainly be a part of your life. As we discussed in Chapter 3, it's important to stimulate your body to stay in the best shape possible—the same holds true for your sex life.

Sex and Sensuality

Life is sensual; we are sensual beings. Sensuality enriches the soul as much as it enriches the body and mind. It is grand in its breadth and scope. The five senses—touch, taste, hearing, sight, and smell—can wrap you up in an intimacy that reaches a dimension outside yourself. You draw life in as you are nourished by a lover and nourish in return.

When your senses are engaged in the many ways available to you, when the inhibitions and fears you had when you were younger have given way to relaxation and understanding, your physical relationship can take on a whole new meaning. Exploring the five senses is a great way to keep your sexuality young and vital.

The Importance of Touch

Your senses are there for you to use, even if the physical act of making love isn't as easy as it once was. Touch is particularly important in times such as this. A tender caress or a relaxing massage can do wonders for both partners. Touch nourishes and heals as much as it comforts and reassures. I can't emphasize the importance of the art—yes, art—of touching enough.

Indulge your sense of touch. Treat yourself and your partner to a massage or, better yet, indulge in a couple's massage. Buy some nice, satiny sheets or a soft wool blanket, and enjoy the way it feels against your skin. Indulge in some scented lotions or oils and see how they feel on your skin, or enjoy the sensation of rubbing them on your partner's body. Take a cool bath together on a hot day, and enjoy the way the water feels on your bodies.

Hold hands in the movie theater, touch your partner's shoulder when expressing gratitude or appreciation, and (everyone's favorite) run your fingers through his hair—or caress his bald scalp. Put your hand in his pocket while waiting in line. These gestures shouldn't be wasted on the young. Intimate strokes and soft caresses are the moments of touch.

A Matter of Taste

Sharing a meal with a cherished partner or friend is another way to engage your senses and foster intimacy. Inhaling the delicious aromas, sipping a glass of wine, and spending time with friends and loved ones is truly one of life's greatest pleasures. The simple act of being together, of opening up to each other in meaningful conversation and hearty laughter, has a warming and relaxing effect. Appreciating the humor in life as you share your experiences encourages intimacy. It is in the act of sharing, being together, and giving each other undivided attention, that you open the door to your inner selves and invite intimacy in. When you share your thoughts and make yourself available to others, you are allowing and encouraging them to do the same. This is how you connect, and I believe that connection is the key element to creating a rich and happy life.

Take the time to have dinner together. Linger over a long meal and talk about your day. Establish a rule not to talk about your jobs or your family for a few hours and try to focus on one another instead. Make a meal that has particular importance to you—perhaps it's something you used to cook together when you were poor newlyweds or that reminds you of a nice vacation you once took. Have dinner at a fancy restaurant as you did when you were dating. Feed each other dessert—be playful. And if some whipped cream or chocolate sauce follows you into the bedroom, so be it!

Food is not only about taste; it engages other senses such as smell and touch. Different foods have different textures that you can react to positively, neutrally, or negatively, and the combination of texture and taste makes a big difference as to how much you enjoy eating. Similarly, the taste of your partner's lips is one of the most intimate tastes in the world. You can identify him blindfolded not only because of how he tastes but how his lips feel on your mouth, neck, or shoulders. When you increase your understanding of how taste in all areas of your life can influence your other senses, sensuality reaches new levels. Have fun and experiment.

The Sounds of Love

Few things spark your imagination the way music does. It has the power to speak to your soul, to light up your heart, to fuel your energy, to bring back a flood of memories, and to help create new ones. It can charge you up as you race into a new day and relax you at the end of it. Music transports you into a mood of intimacy as it feeds and awakens your senses. Nothing sets or communicates a mood the way music can, and nothing else speaks of romance the way music tends to.

The same can be said for the written word, especially when it is read aloud, whether it's great literature, a love letter, or a fantasy. Few things are more romantic or touch the heart as deeply as a poem written to your beloved. The more personal and original, the better. It needn't be Emily Dickinson or Robert Browning; the expression of feelings is what matters, the caring and thought that went into the act of writing itself. Consider the way it says, "I love you" or "I want you." Any woman will tell you that a poem or a love letter—even if it's only those three little words scrawled on a cocktail napkin—will capture her heart (yet, a little blue box from Tiffany's is always welcome, too!). She will also say that this type of foreplay leads to the greatest and most satisfying sexual encounters of all.

Play some of your favorite old records or music that reminds you of a particular time in your life. Go to a concert together, or sing a song the two of you used to love.

It's not only music that can make you relax and put you in a romantic mood. Recite a poem to your partner, one that conveys your true inner self. Tell him how attractive you find him, how handsome he still is after all these years, what specific parts of him—his strong arms, his head of hair, his calloused hands—you find most attractive. Be a bit daring and share a sexual fantasy with him, or tell him how you've been thinking about him all day and what you imagined the two of you doing together that evening.

No matter where you live, there are always new sounds—or sometimes a lack of sound—when you go on vacation. A beach vacation gives you the rhythm of waves hypnotically rolling in to the shore, whereas a vacation in the city provides the hustle and bustle of action and excitement emanating from the streets. The different sounds alone remind you that you are in a new environment and give you an opportunity to explore your reactions to these sounds. Coming in from a day on the beach or back from a Broadway show imprints new sounds and memories on your conscious and subconscious mind. The lapping waves can relax you and set the scene for a romantic evening just as the symphony of the city can. It's what you make of whatever setting you're in.

Beauty and the Eye of the Beholder

Sight is a powerful sense when it comes to sexuality. For some, looking into one another's eyes or simply noticing the allure of a five o'clock shadow is enough to arouse. Others are visually inspired by the curve of a muscle or the way hair falls across a lover's face. We all have our favorites.

What you take in visually on any given day can have such an impact on your moods and emotions that by time you get home, sensory overload has taken over. Reduce the overload by focusing on a simple yet favorite visual. Maybe it's a photograph or painting you love. Allow yourself a moment to just sit and look at it. Think about the calming emotions the image evokes and allow the positive energy to replace the mayhem of the day. Meditation often uses an object, such as a flickering candle, as a visual reference to promote focus. It's calming and sensory overload can melt away in minutes, changing your mood and refocusing your needs.

Indulge your sense of sight by going to a movie together or driving up to the top of a mountain and sitting silently, soaking up the view and the natural beauty all around you. Perhaps go to the local video store and rent a romantic or sexually explicit movie—enjoy watching it together, and see where it takes you. Buy some clothes that make you look and feel sexy, dim the lights a little bit, and let your partner get in the mood by looking at you.

The Surprising Allure of Smell

Walk by a bakery and your nose is immediately engaged by the mouthwatering aroma of baked goods. Enter a forest after a rainstorm where the scent of damp pine lingers. These are just a few of the stimuli that entice the sense of smell. They are strong and powerful ways of awakening one of the most underestimated senses. Most scents don't register because you've become used to them: your home, car, office, clothing, perfume, daily body lotion, and so on. But when you're introduced to a fragrance that you haven't encountered before or in a while, you are reminded of the power of smell. Use this to your advantage.

We've discussed the aroma of meals, lotions, oils, and candles, which are quite common. But aromas like the bakery and the forest illustrate other scents that can be quite sensual as well. Some related smells even have contrasting results—the smell of coffee brewing is delicious, whereas the smell of coffee breath isn't nearly as desirable. What might be alluring to one person can also be a turnoff for another. There's a reason realtors suggest potpourri or air fresheners when holding an open house, but even those scents can offend some people.

Going back to the beach and city vacations, trips introduce scents as well as sounds you may not have experienced in a while: the salt tang of the ocean, delectable city restaurants, flowers from a street vendor, candles from a specialty shop. They all take you out of your usual aroma zone and reawaken and arouse your sense of smell. Tying this sense with any or all of your others adds a wonderful layer to a sensual experience.

The Chemistry Factor

The power of chemistry between two people can't be denied when it's there. Without it, everything else falls by the wayside. It's an inexplicable magic that draws the two of you together, a force that can't be defined or ignored: the electricity that crackles through to the core of your being at the sound of your lover's voice or the moments when laughter crinkles his eyes. It is the fire in a touch, the warmth of an embrace creating the magical something that makes making love the wondrous and beautiful thing it is. This magic may seem to slip away with the passage of time, but it never disappears entirely in a strong and loving relationship. It simply lies dormant, ready to spring to life again when given proper attention.

To appreciate your partner involves saying, "I love you"; showing your feelings in a thousand little ways; and never taking each other for granted. Women especially never tire of hearing those three little words. Maybe it's a Mars and Venus thing, but women desire and need validation while men tend to thrive on genuine support and appreciation. It's only human to want to know that you are needed, valued, and loved. I never hang up the phone with a family member or close friend without saying, "I love you." To me, it's important to always let them know how valued they are and how much I treasure having them in my life.

Everything discussed in this book is an important component to sexuality. If you are fit and strong, you feel sexier. If you have self-confidence, you feel sexier. If you feel good about your body, faults and all, and are tuned in to your own sensuality, you definitely feel sexier. If you are open and loving and have a good sense of humor, that's sexy. Power is sexy. Success is sexy. Glamour is sexy. So are honesty, vulnerability, tenderness, sweetness, and enthusiasm. Nothing is sexier or more desirable than a lover who truly needs and desires you and whom you truly need and desire in return. Find what works between the two of you and continuously explore these and other ways to keep your love (and love life) alive.

Sexuality is really about the way in which you open up to someone else and connect on the deepest level. It's when you move outside yourself and into the realm of a lover that your most meaningful connections take place. When you care more about someone else than you do about yourself. When you're no longer as concerned with the outcome as you are with the journey. If fireworks go off at the end of the road, so much the better; if not, that's fine, too. The act of intimacy becomes so important: the touching, the caring, the tenderness, the sense of adventure, the trust you have in one another, looking into each other's eyes and realizing yet again how very lucky you are to have each other and to be giving yourselves in this way. Surrender yourself and try not to be afraid of attempting something new; when you do, if it turns out to be awkward or just plain doesn't work out, laugh about it. Life is often funny, and so is human sexuality. Again, it's about love and laughter, of allowing humor and happiness to bubble up and create your joy.

Chapter 7

Finishing Touches

B eauty is a greater recommendation than any letter of introduction.

—Aristotle

I'm often asked about my beauty routine, a topic that makes my kids laugh because their first thought is of me with wild, unkempt hair—a sight they've seen plenty of times over the years. I do have a routine that uses my preferred hair and skin products, is fairly simple, and works consistently for me now, but it has changed over the years as I've aged. One of the most important things to realize when it comes to beauty is that it's not about the amount of money you spend as much as it is about finding the products that work best for your skin and hair type and combining those products to achieve the best results. It's very important to understand that skin and hair change as you age, so always watch for the time when products no longer work well and be willing to make changes. As hard as it is to admit, it may be time to say good-bye to the soap you've been using for the past twenty years.

It's not only what products you choose that's important; the key is how you *apply* a product. For example, a twenty-year-old applies makeup with a much different goal than a sixty-year-old. When you're young, you put on makeup to be noticed and to enhance what nature has already provided. But as you grow older, you use makeup to enhance your good features, play down noticeable defects such as under-eye circles or uneven coloring, and maintain a healthy and radiant appearance. A younger woman's advantages are plump, pink lips; rosy cheeks; bright eyes; smooth skin; and glossy hair. When you age, you need to overcome the natural fading of these characteristics by applying the right products.

Skin Care

Oh, to have the skin you had when you were twenty. Sadly, that's not going to happen anytime soon. The fact is, aging is unavoidable, but there are things you can do to keep your skin—and the rest of your face—looking young and healthy. Before we talk about that, let's hear some facts on why skin ages the way it does from my dear friend, Alberto Pena, M.D.

As you approach your thirties, your body's production of collagen and elastin (two substances that give your skin its firmness and elasticity) begins to slow down. The collagen and elastin also begin to loosen and unravel, which results in skin that is looser and less supple. At the same time, fat cells beneath the skin may begin to disappear. With this loss of supportive fat, collagen, and elastin, plus the pull of gravity, the skin begins to sag and form wrinkles. It also loses the ability to moisturize itself and retain moisture, leading to dryness, possibly with itchy, irritated patches.

With age also comes the appearance of those familiar lines and wrinkles that we associate with older skin. Frown lines (the wrinkles between the eyebrows) and crow's feet (lines that radiate from the corners of the eyes) begin to appear as a result of permanent small muscle contractions.

Your Habits and Your Skin

In addition to the natural processes that occur in your body and skin as you age, other long-term habits can cause damage to your skin. You'll want to reduce your exposure to the sun, the most damaging external factor that affects the condition and health of your skin and is the primary cause of premature aging (called photoaging) and skin cancers (including melanoma, basal cell carcinoma, and squamous cell carcinoma). In fact, many of the features associated with older-looking skin are actually caused by sun exposure and not by the natural aging process. Photoaging can cause a number of skin conditions, including:

- ❧ Fine wrinkles
- ❧ Liver spots
- ❧ Dilated blood vessels
- ❧ Rough skin

Smoking is also harmful to your skin. It causes the blood vessels in the top layers of skin to narrow (constrict), which reduces the blood supply, the amount of oxygen available to your skin, and the removal of waste products and dead cells. This process contributes to the reduction in collagen and elastin and prevents vitamin A from bonding with skin cells to repair damage, giving skin a grayish or bluish cast and a leathery texture. Smoking also restricts circulation, taking away the rosy blush of youth. The facial expressions you make when smoking may also cause wrinkles around your lips (pursing around a cigarette) and eyes (squinting to keep out smoke).

One of the most important things you can do for your skin is to eat a diet high in antioxidants and omega-3 fatty acids.

Salmon, tuna, mackerel, and lake trout are all high in natural omega-3 oils. Leafy green vegetables and brightly colored fruits are great sources of antioxidants: spinach, broccoli, tomatoes, strawberries, and blueberries are all excellent choices. The deeper the color, the better it is for you.

Common Signs of Aging

When skin ages and accumulates damage from sun and other habits, a number of skin conditions may result, including the following:

- **Lentigines.** Also known as age or liver spots, lentigines are flat, brown spots that usually show up on the face, hands, back, and feet. These spots are not dangerous (and are not a sign of liver disease). If, however, you notice a dark, flat area with irregular (not rounded) borders, see a dermatologist to ensure that it is not a melanoma.

- **Bruises.** Older skin bruises more easily than younger skin and takes a much longer time to heal. Bruises that don't heal after a week or so should be examined by a dermatologist.

- **Wrinkles.** As skin becomes less elastic, it begins to sag, particularly around the eyes, mouth, forehead, and cheeks.

- **Telangiectasias.** Often called broken capillaries, telangiectasias are visible, dilated blood vessels in the face, usually caused by sun damage.

↜ **Actinic keratoses.** These are rough, warty, reddish, or brownish growths caused by sun damage. They are often precursors to squamous cell carcinomas (skin cancer).

↜ **Cherry angiomas.** These red, protruding growths on the body are caused by dilated blood vessels. They are harmless and occur in about 85 percent of people past middle age.

↜ **Seborrheic keratoses.** These are brown or black raised spots or warty growths on the skin's surface.

Good Habits for Your Skin
It's best to start protecting your skin during childhood, but you can always begin to take the necessary precautions to help protect it, keep it looking young and healthy, and hopefully slow down the effects of aging. Following are some tips on achieving younger looking skin:

↜ **Minimize sun exposure.** Cutting down on the amount of sun your skin gets is the most important thing you can do to protect it and keep it looking young. Wear sunscreen of at least SPF 15 when outdoors, and protect your face with a brimmed hat. Try to stay out of the sun from approximately 10:00 A.M. to 4:00 P.M., which is the most hazardous time for ultraviolet exposure.

↜ **Protect your skin from dryness.** Aging skin can be dry, flaky, and itchy. Use a moisturizer containing petrolatum or lanolin immediately after bathing. Also, use mild soaps and cleansers. Consider bathing less often and using warm water to bathe rather than hot water, which can be more drying.

ક્ષ **Drink plenty of water.** Drinking water throughout the day ensures proper hydration and helps reduce skin dryness. Doctors and nutritionists recommend drinking at least six to eight glasses every day.

ક્ષ **Eat a healthy diet.** Eating a balanced diet will benefit your body as well as your skin. Fruits and vegetables are particularly important for preventing premature skin aging, because they contain many antioxidants.

ક્ષ **Exercise.** Exercise promotes capillary function, which can decrease premature aging. It also increases oxygen to the tissues, which keeps skin looking young and healthy.

ક્ષ **Stop smoking.** Quitting smoking at any age reduces further damage to your skin.

Products That Can Help

The following are some common active ingredients in over-the-counter products that can help keep your skin looking young and healthy:

ક્ષ **Alpha hydroxy acids (AHAs).** These acids produce a mild sloughing (peeling) action that takes off the top layer of skin and exposes the fresher skin underneath. AHAs are usually derived from fruit or dairy products (the latter are sometimes called lactic acid), and many facial moisturizers now contain them.

- **Retinol.** A form of vitamin A, retinol is contained in many skin creams and may temporarily cause your skin to swell slightly, reducing the appearance of fine lines and wrinkles.

- **Antioxidants.** Topical antioxidants such as vitamins C and E can help cells repair the damage caused by the sun's ultraviolet radiation and smoking. This can help skin appear smoother and more glowing.

- **Ammonium lactate.** A combination of lactic acid and ammonium hydroxide, ammonium lactate is used to clear up dry, scaly patches.

- **Ceramide.** This substance is beginning to play a large part in the manufacturing of creams intended to make skin look younger. Ceramide helps skin hang on to its natural moisturizing lipids and helps reduce damage to skin cells.

- **Ginkgo biloba.** This natural herbal concentrate does not have scientific backing but claims to increase circulation, making skin appear rosier and clearer.

- **Tretinoin.** This substance is related to vitamin A and retinol. Tretinoin cream, currently available only by prescription, can be used on your face to treat acne, fine wrinkles, rough skin, and mottled pigmentation.

∽∽∽ A Healthy Skin Regimen ∽∽∽

Nuturing healthy skin is actually a relatively simple process. It's as easy as cleansing properly, exfoliating, and moisturizing, with the option of wearing makeup, if you'd like.

Step 1: Clean Your Skin

When it comes to skin care, I've always washed my face every morning and evening. I feel that I need a clean, smooth surface on which to apply my makeup in the morning and that it's even more important to remove the day's grime and cosmetics before bedtime. I remove my makeup with Ponds Clean Sweep towelettes and then wash with a mild cleanser (never soap). Cetaphil, available in any drugstore, is a great mild cleanser. (The same company also makes a wonderful body moisturizer that comes in a jar. I slather it on after every shower.) Be careful not to use anything too abrasive or with any harsh chemicals or fragrances. When washing your face, remember, less is more.

Step 2: Exfoliate and Tone

I am a firm believer in exfoliating. It removes the dead surface layer of skin cells to uncover the glowing skin beneath. I remember hearing Christie Brinkley say in an interview that she can't exfoliate enough and nodding my head in agreement. A gentle exfoliation every day or every other day will make your skin appear younger and healthier and give it a dewy look. There are many gentle exfoliating creams on the market, and you should poke around to find one that works for you. Remember, gentle is the way to go. Avoid products that claim to provide dermabrasion and microdermabrasion properties, as these are probably too harsh for your skin. I adore Susan Lucci's Youthful Essence line (available online at youthfuless ence.com) and use it on both my face and my body three times per week.

In between exfoliating, I'll also use some toner on my skin to tighten my pores; this helps get rid of some of the discolor- ation that can appear on your skin as you age. I recommend that you use a very mild toner that contains virtually no alco- hol (0 to 10 percent), water, and a humectant such as glycerin. Humectants help prevent moisture from evaporating from the upper layers of your skin. Rose water is a natural and wonder- fully fragrant toner.

Skin tonics are slightly stronger and contain a small quan- tity of alcohol (up to 20 percent), water, and a humectant. Orange flower water is an example of a skin tonic. These prod- ucts are suitable for use on normal, combination, and oily skin but tend to be harsher than toners.

I recommend that you avoid harsh astringent toners. These are very strong and contain a high proportion of alcohol (20 to 60 percent), antiseptic ingredients, water, and a humectant. They are commonly recommended for oily skin because they are drying, but note that removing oil from your skin can lead to excess oil production as your skin tries to compensate and prevent moisture loss. Witch hazel is an example of an astrin- gent. To prevent dehydration, astringent is best applied only to problem areas of skin, such as blemishes.

I tend to use Clinique Toner #3 or #4 because it makes my skin smooth and gets rid of dead-cell buildup (which interferes with applying makeup and creams effectively) without damag- ing my skin.

Step 3: Moisturize, Moisturize, Moisturize

With advancing age, skin can lose essential moisture, resulting in age spots, wrinkles, and dullness. Dry skin also slows down the healing of any small cuts or abrasions. Many moisturizers on the market are specially designed to give your skin immediate luminosity and minimize the appearance of age spots and wrinkles with light-diffusing properties. Since it is essential to protect your skin from the sun, make sure that your moisturizer has an SPF value of 15 or higher.

While most people understand the importance of moisturizing their skin, it's just as important to use the right moisturizer. In the winter, choose a cream rather than a lotion, and look for ones that are fragrance free. Also, be sure to apply moisturizer immediately after your shower while your skin is still damp, as well as before and after spending time in the cold air.

Step 4: Make Sure the Eyes Have It

Another essential part of my antiaging skin care routine is eye cream. There are numerous creams and unguents to choose from, and they are a good investment—they really can help drooping skin and lessen the appearance of wrinkles around your eyes. I use Age Defy's Revercel Eye Perfection Serum with Retinol (agedefy.com), but any cream that has a bit of AHA and retinol is fine.

Step 5: Add the Extras

I admit it—I don't like to leave the house without putting on just a touch of makeup. I had great skin when I was younger; my cheeks were naturally rosy and my complexion was smooth and even. Now I need a bit more help.

It's important not to overdo makeup as you get older—as difficult as it is, you have to learn to accept your hard-earned wrinkles, uneven skin tone, and dry or oily skin. Sometimes when I'm at a photo shoot with younger models, I can't help but marvel at how gorgeous and unlined their faces are without any makeup at all. And while I wouldn't trade in my wrinkles of wisdom for the world, I don't mind using a little makeup here and there to help make me look and feel a bit more youthful and attractive. Heed the advice of Lauren Hutton: "That's the mistake women make—you shouldn't see your makeup. We don't want to look like we've made an effort."

I like using a light foundation (Yves St. Laurent's oil-free formula) to give my face more balance and then use light mascara and an eyebrow pencil; well-shaped eyebrows frame your eyes and can make all the difference in your face. If your skin has grown paler with age and your hair a little (or in my case, a lot) whiter, it can have the overall effect of making you look washed out. So even just a touch of color to offset the color of your eyes or emphasize a nice brow line can really enhance the way you look. Eyebrow specialist Anastasia Soare of Anastasia Beverly Hills has been on "Oprah" several times and is known for saying, "My goal is to make the eyebrows beautifully symmetrical because even when features are asymmetrical—as they most often are—well-shaped brows will bring a kind of harmony to the face." Her products are available online at anastasia.net. You can get advice on the proper shaping and care of your brows at many salons, so take advantage of them. As you age, the best shape and color for your brows might change since your skin and muscle tone alter.

I use a soft pink lipstick with a touch of gloss over it. Some authorities disagree and recommend reds or corals to enliven your face. As with all makeup, you should aim to look your age, only better. Heavy, sharp, or bright red lipstick might be fine when you are in your twenties and thirties, but when you're older, it can look cartoonish.

∽Hair: The Crowning Jewel∽

I highlighted my light brown hair from my twenties through my fifties until it started turning whiter and whiter across the top. Finally, in my early sixties, I just let the white take over and haven't looked back. I'm fortunate that the shade is becoming to my skin tone, and I am often stopped in the street by women who want to know who colors my hair. I tell them, "Nature." If it weren't such a great color, I would certainly add something to correct and improve it. Don't be afraid of letting your hair go gray or white as long as the color enlivens your face. Your hairdresser can advise you as to which products are good for white or gray hair. If you choose to color it, follow the same rules as you would with makeup by using a clear, subtle color that works with your skin and hair texture. Deep black, bright red, or brassy blonde is best left to those in their twenties or thirties. Strive for mellow brown, auburn, and blonde.

In terms of products, I use Bumble & Bumble (B&B) or Kérastase shampoo and conditioner, but any store-bought shampoo or conditioner will do.

My hair has some natural wave, which helps with styling (though I still tease my hair lightly to keep it from falling in my face). I only need to wash it every few days, but when I do wash and style it, I strive to keep the time that it takes to a minimum. My routine consists of washing with either B&B Thickening Shampoo followed by the seaweed conditioner or Kérastase shampoo and conditioner. I towel dry it before adding a bit of

B&B Styling Crème. I blow-dry it with my head upside down to add volume and then put in huge Velcro rollers (found in any drugstore) on the top and sides. I use a large round brush on the back and go over everything with the dryer. While the rollers sit, I do my makeup (every minute counts) and then brush out and style my hair, finishing with a light hair spray. My hair tends to be soft and fine, and living directly on the Pacific Ocean, having a good hair day is a challenge. Dealing with fog and dampness is my personal nemesis, but a fat curling iron with a one-and-a-half-inch barrel works wonders in undoing the damage and getting rid of the frizz. When I'm in a rush and don't have time to fuss, I pull my hair back in a ponytail and am on my way.

I've allowed my hair to remain long over the years. It is now shoulder length because that works well for me, but you should find a style that is flattering to your face, height, and build. Never choose what you think you should wear because you're a certain age. A good cut is always critical so your hair will fall back into place even after you're out on a windy day. A flattering cut combined with suitable color and products that keep your hair manageable and healthy will ensure that you always look your best.

Special Advice for Thinning Hair

Here are some questions that women often have regarding their thinning hair.

Q. *What length of cut best hides thinning hair?*
A. Shorter cuts—above the shoulder—work best to camouflage thinning hair, although the best

length also depends on hair's texture and overall style. Short or medium-length hair that's curly can be cut in layers. Wavy hair can be cut medium length or long, whereas straight hair can be given volume with flattering graduated layers around the face or a blunt cut. Too many layers can look thinner than a blunt cut, so be careful not to overlayer. Talk to your stylist.

Q. *Are some colors better than others at hiding thin hair?*

A. Lighter shades that are closer to your skin tone work best to camouflage thinning hair. Darker shades tend to show a greater contrast, thereby exaggerating the condition.

Q. *Does coloring or highlighting my hair contribute to further thinning?*

A. Experts say that hair thinning is caused by a genetic condition called androgenetic alopecia. Since coloring and highlighting are applied externally to the hair shaft, these processes do not contribute to further thinning. If your hair loss is especially bad, you may wish to consult your health care provider before coloring your hair.

Q. *I'm afraid to go into a salon because I am embarrassed by my thinning hair. What should I do?*

A. Don't be worried at all. Most stylists are familiar with all kinds of hair textures and conditions and know the best cuts, colors, and treatment options to help you manage your fine or thinning hair. Remember that your stylist is a professional and is there to help you and offer you advice on how to look your best.

Q. *It doesn't seem to matter if I part my hair to the left or the right—it still shows my scalp. What should I do?*

A. Try cutting your hair short and wearing a "messy" style, or try a zigzag part. If your hair is straight, layer the top (or the whole thing) and then set it with curlers to camouflage the thinning. You can also try combing your hair back with no part.

Q. *Does exposure to the sun make hair loss worse?*

A. No, but it is a good idea to protect your scalp from the sun with a hat or sunscreen.

Q. *Are there special shampoos or conditioners I should use?*

A. There are many volumizing shampoos and conditioners on the market that will help to plump up fine hair, and some of them may also help the appearance of thinning hair. Also, products containing panthenol and herbs such as jasmine, angelica, and willow will keep your hair looking full and healthy. You should use a shampoo that cleanses your scalp well and a conditioner that is light and won't weigh hair down. Progaine is a line of products that addresses the needs of women with fine and thinning hair.

Q. *Does blow-drying my hair contribute to its thinning?*

A. No, but sometimes the hair is delicate, so use low heat and less tension. Extreme heat and hard pulling will damage your hair and cause breakage.

Q. *I want to use Rogaine for women to treat my thinning hair. How do I incorporate it into my styling regimen?*

A. You can continue to style and care for your hair the same way you always have. Women's Rogaine needs to remain on your scalp for about four hours, so if you're going to wash your hair, wash it and towel it dry before applying the Rogaine to your scalp. Wait for the product to dry, and then just style your hair as you normally would.

Q. *How does Women's Rogaine affect my hairstyle? Does it make my hair greasy?*

A. It has the consistency of water and is applied only to your scalp. Using it twice daily as directed should not affect your hairstyle or make your hair greasy.

❧ Dressing Well ☙

The way you dress is a strong reflection not just of your body, but of your mind and soul as well. Dressing to accentuate your body is what you consider first when buying clothes. Yet no matter how good something may look on you, you also need to be comfortable inside. It is the totality that puts your mind at ease so you think and feel that you are dressed right. Whether it's an interview, a cocktail party, a charity event, or just running to the grocery store, when you're dressed properly, you feel content and confident. When you feel satisfied about how you look, your mind and soul reflect these feelings and your interactions with others become easier. You express all aspects of your true self.

Everyone tries to choose a look that works for them. For me, it's always been a classic style. This look is ageless and you can't go wrong with it, but naturally there are those who opt for more flair. Just be careful that your look doesn't date or misplace you. You want to dress appropriately for your age. As women get older, they sometimes fool themselves into thinking that if they dress "young," they will look younger, but they actually look older. Magazines like *Vogue* and *Harper's Bazaar* have plenty of tips on dressing appropriately for your age, often showing looks for different decades in life. Both my modeling and public relations careers require me to be on the ball mentally and to look the part. Fortunately, I've always loved fashion (a trait inherited from my mother) and piecing clothing items together to create my classic look. I use the added flair of accessories to make my look unique. A wardrobe full of basic black, beige, and white with some touches of color is all I've ever needed to acquire the look I want for work, play, or evening.

Fitting in at Work

It's actually pretty easy to maintain my wardrobe. The racks of my closet are filled with basic, well-cut jackets and blazers of the best-quality fabrics I can afford (I often pick these up on sale at high-end department stores and boutiques). You don't need to buy many pieces, but always opt for the best quality your budget can handle. The clothes will last for years. My personal favorites, because they are cut right for my shape, are from Ralph Lauren and Armani Collezioni. For my tall, fairly straight figure, I always opt for a curvy riding-jacket cut that nips in at the waist and accentuates my hips. Boxy doesn't work on my tall, narrow frame. Alternatives to the riding jacket are short, fitted little jackets (they can be made of anything from denim to velvet) with interesting details. Study your body and figure out the shapes that look best on you. Women's lifestyle and fashion magazines can be great resources for this type of evaluation.

Don't be shy about asking salespeople for assistance. They might pick out something you'd never consider, but when you try it on, it looks fabulous and feels just right. Personally, no matter who recommends it, I never wear anything with a print because I don't like prints on me. (This actually allows me to mix and match my clothes more readily, too.) In short, have your mind open to suggestion but stick with what instinct tells you works best for you.

Pairing jackets and blazers with solid, well-fitting pants (they can even be khakis), a classic shirt, and simple jewelry provides a clean look for work. Try slacks in lightweight wools with some stretch to them and flat fronts—no pleats. One look I've learned to avoid is anything with too high a waist; nothing will age or date you faster. With most pants cut so low nowadays, the challenge is to find something in between. This is especially difficult when it comes to buying jeans, but with a little sleuthing and perseverance, you can find them. I prefer Victoria's Secret London Jeans and J. Brand. When I discover a brand that works particularly well for dress or work, I'll buy the same style in a couple of different colors.

It is important to always make sure that your clothes fit well. No matter how nicely you're shaped, a piece of clothing you just love may not show you off to your best advantage. If it doesn't fit properly, a seamstress at your local cleaners is an invaluable source for making necessary adjustments and is often no more expensive than what you would pay for one or two dry cleanings. It's worth it if the item is one that you'll wear often. Occasional tailoring is not a luxury; it's a necessity. Don't forget, the aim is to have a garment you will wear for years.

Having a long (size 10), narrow foot can sometimes make it hard to find shoes. I prefer pumps that look feminine, with pointed toes and a low heel, but I'll go higher for dressier occasions. High heels are great for making your legs look longer. Clunky or heavy shoes don't work with my look, and they break up a sleek, classic line.

One thing that is universal to all of us, particularly as we age, is how to camouflage the effects of menopause on our tummies, arms, and legs. As much as we may try to deny them, there they are—those annoying little bulges, the arms that threaten to flap if a stiff wind comes up, and the unwelcome appearance of cellulite here and there. The truth is that we can't wish or even exercise them away, but we can do a lot to cover them up and distract attention from them. When you're putting your wardrobe together, *don't* make the mistake of thinking that something large and baggy will cover you up and make you look smaller or thinner. Just the opposite is true. Again, well-cut, properly fitted clothes that accentuate your positives and at least hide, if not eliminate, your negatives are the key. If your hips are generous, select clothes that minimize rather than draw attention to them. For example, choose jackets, sweaters, and tops that extend down below the hips, thereby covering the offending area. Anything that draws attention to your upper body and face is good. Small shoulder pads in your jacket will give you width across the top, thus balancing the hip area and making it less noticeable.

Go for simple sheaths or A-line dresses that give you a smooth, slimmer look. If you have a small waist and like to accentuate it, choose a fuller skirt that goes down to or below your knees. Pair it with a fitted jacket for a great day or evening look. When shopping for pants, avoid pleats like the plague and go for a nice flat front. Magazines are filled with excellent tips and suggestions on how to dress for your build, and several talk shows and cable programs cover this topic regularly.

Another key factor is properly fitting undergarments, particularly bras. Enlist the help of a specialist in a lingerie store because most of us are not nearly as knowledgeable on this subject as we think we are. Believe me, the right bra can make all the difference in how your clothes look and fit. There are wonderful options out there for minimizing, maximizing, or just making the best of your already just-right bust size.

One more tip while we're on the subject of undergarments: never forget the importance of indulging in some beautiful, sexy lingerie. Wearing silk or lace under almost anything, whether jeans or a business suit, acts as a lovely reminder of your sensual, feminine side. Maybe you won't want to do it every day, but make it an important option at least once in a while.

Weekend Solutions

I often work weekends—meeting guests for breakfast or dinner, attending a tournament, or going to a modeling job—but even on my time off, my look is normally a more casual version of my work outfits. My favorites are fitted jeans or khakis with a classic shirt, sweater, or jacket. I have some great-looking, fitted fleece jackets in scrumptious colors from Gorsuch (stores throughout Colorado or catalog orders). I pair these with casual or sporty pants in a straight cut—nothing baggy—in black or white, perfect for a walk on the beach, visiting grandchildren, or grocery shopping.

Evening Glamour

For evenings out, I prefer a figure-flattering cocktail suit or a little black dress. On the occasions that I wear a coat for a dressy evening, it's made of an expensive-looking fabric; velvet and brocade are luxurious and glamorous at formal events.

Overall, I have found that it's not necessary to have a large closet full of clothes. I definitely believe that we wear 10 percent of our clothes 90 percent of the time. Don't buy something unless you are absolutely in love with it, and when you do bring home something new, try to get rid of at least one, if not two, items in your closet by donating them or selling them at a consignment shop if they are in good enough condition. Having a small number of great choices is what's important.

They don't need to be expensive choices. The cut and fit are what count. Some of the greatest looking classics come from inexpensive stores—think white shirts from The Gap.

Beautiful Accessories

Accessories are what make any outfit. Without them a blazer is just a blazer, a top is just a top. Your personal accessory choices are what define you as a unique individual. To keep in line with my classic look, I work in a few solid gold or sterling silver pieces—earrings, bracelets, and necklaces that can be worn as signature pieces. We each cultivate our own signature by wearing pieces that identify us. Gold is great, as are pearls; if it works with your coloring, silver can be very elegant. Over the years, I've mixed some great-looking faux pieces with good jewelry. Not only are the costume pieces fun, but no one can tell the difference—especially if you're properly dressed and you look as if you always wear the real thing.

While I don't wear chunky shoes, I love chunky, handsome, one-of-a-kind jewelry that's fun and rounds out my collection. Many designers around the country make very handsome costume jewelry that's usually available in high-end department stores and boutiques. These items can be signature or statement pieces just as well as solid gold, pearls, or silver can. The point here is to mix what you like and be open to style possibilities.

The final touch is the handbag. Again, I use classics; shoulder bags and clutches work best with my wardrobe. Opting for good-quality leather, nothing trendy or too young looking, will make your outfit. Choose something in style (such as a clutch or an envelope, if that's what's "in"), but always pick a simple, elegant look to complement and enhance your head-to-

toe look. In order to be well dressed in the past, your handbag had to match your shoes. Thankfully, those days are over. Now we can be so much more creative and versatile in how we dress because we have so many wonderful options open to us. Accessories are so important. You can take an ordinary outfit and turn it into something stylish and interesting just by adding a beautiful scarf, piece of jewelry, shoes, or handbag. If beautiful handbags are your thing, pick one that complements your shoes and outfit, but make it one that also makes a statement about you! And please choose a bag that's not only appropriate for the occasion but also in proportion and flattering to your body type. If you're small, don't go for an oversized bag. If you're a little on the heavy side, pick a bag that's slim and flat.

How you present yourself, especially from the inside out, affects how you feel about yourself and how others receive you. Beauty enhancements, when you're comfortable with them, put you in a positive mind-set, which is always wonderful to have. When we feel and think we're beautiful, others pick up on it, which reinforces this positive feeling. The body and mind are much more connected than we think!

Part 2

The Mind

Chapter 8

A Positive Spin

A straight path never leads anywhere except to the objective.

—André Gide, author

From the moment you wake up and touch your painted toes to the floor, you're starting a new day with new opportunities. The thoughts and mind-set with which you approach that day say a lot about how you can expect it to unfold. Do you hit the snooze and grumble under the weight of your pillow, or do you take a moment and consider all that you're grateful for and have to look forward to? I suggest that you strive for the latter because how you start your day gives credence to the way you'll handle all that it brings you. Remember that life throws you rough times, but it's how you handle them that counts.

The number of books, CDs, and movies about the power of positive thinking grows daily, and I think that's wonderful. More and more people are benefiting and learning from teachings about the power of creation and the manifestation of healthy, happy, and spiritually abundant lives, whether from such early authors as Florence Scovel Shinn and Norman Vincent Peale or today's contributors to Rhonda Byrne's *The Secret*. This extremely popular book's message is that by immersing yourself in three steps—(1) ask the universe for what you want, (2) believe that you are already receiving it, and (3) settle back, relax, and receive it—you have the power to create your dreams. Byrne's philosophy (and that of many others) draws strongly on the power of visualization, positive energy, and gratitude. She is not alone in this. Oprah Winfrey has talked for years about the power of keeping a gratitude journal, and Deborah Norville has a popular book out on the subject, *Thank You Power*.

While these philosophies are ones that I, in hindsight, have practiced for much of my life, it's refreshing and reassuring to read and hear the enthusiasm in these authors' words and beliefs. In some ways, this is the exciting part of the journey—still discovering, exploring, and realizing that on some level I've had an understanding of these ideas for years; I just didn't know it on a fully conscious level. These authors have put my actions and way of life into words, which in turn has allowed me to formulate my beliefs on a deeper level and share them with others. I've found that you can never reinforce positive behavior, thoughts, and feelings enough.

Positive Thinking

The knowledge and power of positive thinking that I've explored and used successfully during the different phases of my life fascinate me. Author Deepak Chopra has pointed to research that says we have more than sixty-five thousand thoughts per day, and nearly 95 percent of them are the same thoughts we generated the day before. Would you have guessed that you have that many thoughts a day, let alone that you have had them before? I read this and wondered how many of these thoughts are positive rather than negative—having sixty-five thousand positive thoughts sounds like a wonderful thing, whereas having sixty-five thousand negative recurring thoughts sounds absolutely awful. Science has proven that we have the ability to create and shape our life experiences through our thoughts and words. Yet oftentimes we don't realize that the things we visualize or talk about often come to fruition, even if it's not until years later.

Understanding this concept has made me want to constantly fine-tune my thinking toward keeping my thoughts positive, since those are the experiences I want to continue to bring myself. For example, whether I'm driving to work and thinking about the day ahead or cooking dinner at home, I pay attention to my thoughts and consider how optimistic they are, knowing that down the road they will show themselves and I will be happy they were positive. This philosophy flows over to my conversations with people throughout the day. I gauge how positive my words are as I'm talking, which can be hard at times. Having a voice in the back of your mind asking, "Are these words positive?" can feel awkward at first, but in time you grow used to it and the positive thoughts become natural. As time passes, you will start to notice the influence this consciously driven change is having on your life.

When you think about something, you're focusing on whatever it is—an experience, a person, an ambition. Sometimes you start noticing the results immediately. It can be as simple as hearing from an old friend about whom you recently thought. Or possibly you've considered making a career change that you've been working toward for some time and you meet someone at a dinner party who can help you. Maybe you've been dreaming about your ideal retirement town and suddenly your local newspaper runs a travel article raving about it. You are led to the people, places, and experiences with which your mind spends time.

To manifest the wonderful experiences you want in life, it's important to realize that the stronger the emotion you feel toward what you're discussing or thinking, the more likely it will be to manifest. But keep in mind that this works both ways—positive emotions and thoughts manifest just as easily as their negative counterparts. As the old saying goes, "Be careful what you wish for." Fortunately positive thoughts hold much more strength in your convictions, which gives you an edge. For example, if you're excited about an upcoming vacation, the positive emotions you have about it will outweigh any negative doubts that may cross your mind. Think about how easy the flight will be, how you have the perfect hotel room, and how you'll be able to relax and enjoy the sand and surf—or the mountains or the city skyline. No matter where you travel, you're more likely to have a fun-filled vacation if you focus on the good things to come rather than the lines at the airport or traffic on the highway.

Even in your day-to-day routine, it's often possible to choose a positive thought over a negative or fearful one. Taking the car to the shop because you need new tires? Rather than thinking about the amount of money involved, focus on how much easier and safer it will be to drive through snow and rain. Heading to the doctor for your annual checkup? Consider the good news you may receive since you've changed your lifestyle—reduced cholesterol, lower blood pressure. If there is something of concern, be grateful you're seeking the help you need and that there could be good news down the road. Facing long lines at the grocery store or bank? When I'm in long lines, I use this time to do things like update my checkbook (since it's usually handy); that way I don't have to do it when I'm at home and it makes the time in line go faster. Or I take out a little notepad and make my next list, whether it's work tasks or my own personal to-do list. There's no point in being frustrated because the person in front of you can't decide between paper and plastic when you can put the time to positive use.

Of course there is no limitation to the magnitude or simplicity of thoughts and words. No matter what your dream is—such as becoming a writer, photographer, teacher, violinist, chef, or anything else—if it appears in your mind, it will draw the image in your subconscious, and when you eventually follow up with action, the physical reality will form. I believe this is why so many people who have "made it" repeatedly advise, "Never give up on your dreams," when asked for their secret to success. Believing means never giving up. When my daughter Heather made the decision to follow her dream of becoming a writer, many people asked her what her "plan B" was, to which she responded, "I don't have a plan B because if I did, it would mean that I don't believe enough in my plan A." In a short amount of time and through determination, focus, and action, her writing career took off. The basic philosophy is that if you nurture your mind to stay positive and to overcome obstacles and naysayers, your thoughts will manifest into positive outcomes.

As a teenager in boarding school at Rosemary Hall in Greenwich, Connecticut, I cut out pictures of models and taped them to my dorm room wall, creating a collage (I've recently heard this type of thing called a "vision board," which is a much better way of describing it). Certainly some teenage girls still do this, and I'll bet that those who eventually realize their dreams will be the ones who visualized, felt, and believed that they'd achieve their goals and took the steps to make them happen. They didn't look at the pictures they cut out and think, "That's so-and-so's life, not mine." Instead they said, "That will be me someday," and they held true to that belief.

Sometimes you'll hear or read a simple phrase that sticks in your mind. This phrase can form a strong belief that becomes your mantra. One of my favorite examples is "Leap and the net will appear." I strongly believe that great success often involves taking a great risk. Jumping into my new public relations position at Pebble Beach felt very risky to me. It was a completely new venture, and although I felt confident that I could handle it, like anything new, it was rather frightening at first. Striding down the runway in my first fashion show was a brand-new experience, and I may as well have eaten butterflies for breakfast as I was dressed and made up, but in the end it was great fun. Another example came recently when I was approached by a large California university about speaking to a group of students on the topic of living a fulfilled and enriched life in your fifties and sixties. Public speaking was new to me. I was used to working with individuals and small groups of people I'd never met before, but this was quite different. Nevertheless, I knew it was something I wanted to do, so I agreed, and much to my amazement, I found that I loved it. Now I look forward to more opportunities to speak to both younger and older audiences, to share my experiences and whatever wisdom I've acquired along my journey. One of the high points of being able to share my knowledge is stressing that I'm always careful with the beliefs and thoughts I form since they could all come true. Younger people eat this up because they are looking toward a vast future; the same words rejuvenate older people, helping them believe that they still have plenty of time to create positive experiences in their lives.

A can-do attitude is the key to thinking positively. There are times when it's important not to be afraid of taking a risk, whether it's based on a calculated decision or a gut feeling. When opportunities that feel right come along, even if they're something you've never done before, act on your instinct, think positively, and give a resounding, "Yes!" Often the details fall into place once you've taken that first leap of faith. It's your job to believe you can do it, after that you'll be rewarded and shown why going with your beliefs made all the difference. When your stomach doesn't feel right about something, that's your intuition telling your mind not to go forward. When you have a feeling of jubilation, you're excited or tingly, and something feels like the perfect fit, then you know you're on track. Woman's intuition is a remarkable gift and when you are in tune with it, there isn't much you can't accomplish. Have confidence, and the more you test yourself and move out of your comfort zone, the more confident you become.

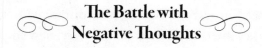

The Battle with Negative Thoughts

It's not always easy to overcome adverse thoughts, especially in your youth when you don't have the experience to recognize them. I grew up in the shadow of Ali McGraw, who was a dear friend during my years at Rosemary Hall. Ali was a year ahead of me and was one of those girls who hopscotched right over the teenage "gawky" stage and went from being a beautiful child to a stunning young woman overnight. Although I imagine she was fighting her own angst at the time, my mind was fraught with typical low self-confidence and I believed I wasn't as beautiful as she was. To make matters worse, I was surrounded by people who had their own ideas of what beauty was, and I was constantly reminded of how gorgeous Ali was by either seeing her or hearing it from everyone else, especially adults. While my self-confidence was an issue for me, my friendship with Ali was fortunately based on many positive and fun times together. The dichotomy presented turned into a love for my friend with some feelings of inferiority I put on myself—a situation many girls at this age face with their friends.

It took time, but with emotional and internal growth I became comfortable with who I was and stopped comparing myself to others. Yet it wasn't until I was in my senior years that I grew to fully believe that I had the potential to be a model, let alone that other people believed it, too. I shed the old negative thoughts and beliefs that were still in my mind and uncovered the hidden desire to be a part of the world I had pasted on my dorm room wall so many years before. Doing this invited in new thoughts and attitudes, which in turn created new and wonderful experiences.

Part of my success in accomplishing my goals ties into my efforts to make everything I do look easy, even if it is extremely difficult for me behind the scenes. I have never played into the role of victim, and I take responsibility for my actions. When you strive to be in control of your life and begin to take charge, you'll be amazed by what you start to create and will want to continue the process. Part of developing this trait is to recognize others who have cultivated the same knack. For example, a writer does not share a first draft, and the second or third often goes unseen as well. A photographer showcases only samples of his finest work and tosses aside the over- or underexposed photographs. A thirty-second television commercial may take two or more days to shoot. Things that look simple are really the result of a great deal of organization and planning. The same is true of raising children, running a household, and throwing a party.

Early on, I mastered the art of continuously showing or trying to show my best self in all that I did. From raising six children to promoting Pebble Beach to strutting the catwalk, I felt that I needed to be my best. In reflection, it may be because I was the daughter of a glamorous mother who demonstrated this for me or because I had the pressures of being Ali's friend during puberty. Ali didn't seem to face the issues that many of us did—acne, oily hair, and so on. In our eyes, she went immediately from child to woman. As her friend, I admired her for her beauty, which resonated inside and out. She and I had slumber parties with other students and friends, visited each other's homes, and had adventures full of the angst and insecurities that are a natural part of life and growth at that age.

Once we all moved on from boarding school and left the awkward teenage years behind, those matters that had seemed so important became trivial and fell by the wayside. I stepped up and took control of my life and decided who I wanted to be and where I wanted to go. It's never too late to change your way of thinking. It can take time, as anything worth attaining does, but eventually new positive and powerful thoughts become the norm—much like your new workout habits.

Many terrific books address positive thinking and using your thoughts, emotions, and actions to create your life.

Wayne Dyer, Abraham Hicks, Norman Vincent Peale, and James Arthur Ray are just a few of the well-known authors on this subject.

∽∽ Exercises for Thinking Positively ∼∼

Exercises for the mind are a great way to start to change or enhance positive thinking. The following ones are derived from my years of experience and are meant to spark your mind and encourage new thought patterns.

Start Changing the Way You Think Today

"I can't/don't [fill in the blank]." For every "I can't" or "I don't" that you say during the day, there is a positive statement that you could and should say instead. For instance, you're going to a dinner party and waiting for your husband to come home. You might think, "I don't want him to be late." Instead, turn the thought around and think, "I want my husband to be on time." Or say a friend invites you to join her in learning a new hobby (see Chapter 11) and your response is, "Oh, I can't do that," followed by a string of excuses. I challenge you to turn the language around and say, "I can try that." Surprise yourself. It's easy to have a knee-jerk negative reaction to new opportunities, yet these are the situations from which you learn and grow.

Turn a Potential Confrontation into a Positive Experience

We all face them at one time or another, and the word itself makes my skin crawl. Confrontations are unpleasant and in many cases unnecessary. If you know a confrontation is coming down the pipe, practice the conversation beforehand. Envision the other person standing inside a hot-air balloon (yes, a hot-air balloon). Make sure he is settled in and then "watch" the balloon lift off the ground—up, up, and away. Really feel him heading away and leaving. This is a great exercise to take the other person's energy off of you, and you'll be amazed how much less confrontational your conversation will be when the time comes. Repeat this several times, if needed, until you feel the other person's energy lifted off of you.

If a situation erupts during an existing conversation, there's a trick I've used that always helps to calm the other person down without my speaking a word. Imagine a band of gold light beaming down on the other person's head. Keep the stream of light steady; then listen as his voice calms and watch as the person relaxes.

Eliminate Negative Influences

As much as you don't enjoy losing people in your life, there comes a time when letting go of someone who is always down alleviates so much negative energy around you that you can feel like an entirely new person. James Arthur Ray refers to these people as "energy vampires" because they suck the energy from you and leave you drained. Everyone has bad days, and part of being a friend is helping others through rough times. I'm not suggesting you let go of valuable friends (see Chapter 16). It's the people who chronically complain and are not willing to change. These conversations have the potential to drag you down and can really zap your energy. It's as though you're a full cup of water (positive energy) and they're empty cups of water (negative energy); when they bring their empty cups to you (through complaining or an equivalent energy drainer), they end up draining your cup into theirs. But since they aren't used to having a full cup of water (positive energy), they don't know what to do with it once they have it so they turn and pour it down the drain. Now you're both left empty. No one wins. Only you can know which relationships drain your cup, evaluate the value they bring to your life, and decide how much they're holding back your spiritual and mental growth.

Enlist a Friend to Help Keep Your Thoughts on Track
It's one thing to tell yourself that you're going to start thinking in a positive manner, and it's quite another to truly and diligently stick to that determination. Many have allowed themselves to slip into the familiar pattern of doubt and worry, seeing the possibility of a negative outcome just as readily as visualizing success, and it's difficult to change those long-held thought processes. To accelerate your progress with positive thinking, ask a friend to help catch you when you slip. You probably have catchphrases or beliefs that you repeat without even being aware of their underlying negativity, and your friend can catch you when you say them (and vice versa). Having someone to help you when you slip back into negativity can be what puts you over the fence. Of course, you also have to be friendly and fair to your friend when you catch her in a slip. You can even offer a positive alternative to her thought. This can even be silly things, like when you're having lunch and she says, "I can't have a burger because I'm trying to lose weight." Change her sentence to "I'm having a veggie burger because it's healthy." This way there is a positive twist and the energy or focus is on health.

To help keep the positive ball rolling, consider expanding your horizons by performing spontaneous acts of kindness for others and yourself. When you reach out to your friends and family with selfless acts and thoughts, you feel better about yourself. It's when you can give freely and genuinely to others that you often feel the best. See the sidebar for some ideas to get your juices flowing on how you can improve your day by brightening someone else's.

Spontaneous Positive Actions

- Call and compliment someone, or thank her for being in your life.
- Walk your dog and say hi to your neighbors.
- Pull up some weeds in your garden.
- Take a friend out to a movie, preferably a comedy.
- Check on an elderly neighbor and bring lunch.
- Fill a bird feeder.
- Create some art—collages, painting, photography, light landscaping in the yard.
- Listen to your favorite song on your iPod or CD player.
- Volunteer at the local animal shelter or a hospital.
- Send a handwritten thank-you note to someone.
- Visit your favorite boutique and try on a hat or dress.
- Call a friend and sing a song on her voice mail.

Chapter 9

Looking Backward
to Move Forward

All men should strive to learn before they die what they are running from, and to, and why.

—*James Thurber*

Movies are a form of escape. They give us something to do on a rainy Sunday afternoon. They provide us with laughter, tears, and joy, and they can sometimes scare us out of our seats. While growing up my friends and I enjoyed watching Grace Kelly, Marilyn Monroe, Audrey Hepburn, and Natalie Wood light up the screen with their grace and beauty. Their counterparts—Gary Cooper, Humphrey Bogart, and Cary Grant—were equally gorgeous and suave. Whether or not they were role models, these actors and actresses played roles in their movies. Yet you have your own personal life movie that you live and create every day. Over time, your movie encompasses moments of laughter, joy, sorrow, and pain, and the plot takes twists and delivers surprises that you couldn't have seen coming. Imagine, if you will, watching your life movie. What part of your script would you rewrite to create a more graceful or beneficial outcome? What part of the script brings moments of pride? Who were your supporting actors and actresses, and how did they impact your story?

Looking back on the movie of your life is a great way to move forward, as long as you don't remain stuck looking at the screen. Whatever your movie looks like, you are fortunate to have memories and experiences on which to reflect. If a plot twist changed the dynamics of a relationship, living arrangement, or career, you learned from that experience, and it can be helpful to think about that scene again when you're faced with a similar decision. You discover that each loss teaches you that the movie of life doesn't stop for anyone; you can either stop and obsess on one scene while the film keeps moving forward, or you can go with the flow by processing the experience rather than dwelling on it. Some scenes naturally take longer to play out than others. Others might have had more drama and changed a part of you forever. Each love lost teaches you the art of resolve and hopefully lessons about yourself that help you grow. Each decision you've made along the way paved a new path toward your future and now gives you the opportunity to reflect on your successes.

Regardless of the fact that you play the starring role in your personal life movie, you also play a supporting role in the lives of many other people: your spouse, your children, your friends, your colleagues, even the clerk at the grocery store. No matter what those supporting roles were and still are, you learn from being in their movies, too. Yet even as a supporting player, you can sometimes become so involved in the day-to-day role you play that you don't always have a clear view of the big picture for many years, and that view often provides the biggest lessons. For example, a teacher may not realize the influence she's had on a particular student until years later when the student acknowledges her as part of his success. A stranger's kind gesture when you're in need may create a pivotal change in the way you think about or treat others. The end of a relationship can be traumatic, but it leaves the door open for a new one that could be the one you really need and appreciate. Anything from a momentary gesture to a full-blown relationship can be considered a supporting role in your life movie, and each one can have just as big an influence on your thinking and being as the others. I've learned to consider not only other people's influence on my life, but my secondary role in theirs. Maybe it's me who offers the kind gesture that changes someone's paradigm. Maybe it was me who let someone go so he could meet the people he was meant to meet instead. I'm not suggesting dwelling on this concept (there are far too many people and situations), but do keep in mind that every action and word leaves your footprint on other people's lives.

Hindsight is a tool worth using to take a deeper look at your life movie. Doing so in a healthy manner can contribute to your personal growth. For instance, looking back on the role Wally and I played as parents is a very different view than that of some of our children who are now parents; this is due both to our completely different goals and desires as adults and to the different environment our grandchildren are growing up in. Both Wally and I were only children, so having a large family was important to us, yet my sons and daughters who are parents only have a few children. Their movies are quite different, and their children's movies will be as well.

Reflect on the chances you took and the life experiences you passed up along the way. These choices are what molded you into the seasoned being you've become. The beauty of it is that no matter how many gray hairs and wrinkles have been caused by your past, no matter how many scenes went seemingly wrong, the experiences you endured and relished gave you the long-earned life "authority" that you now have. They gave you the knowledge and wisdom to advise and to share what you've learned with those around you.

What Roles Do You Play?

Are you a parent? A coworker? A friend? A doctor? These are just a few examples of the different supporting roles we play in other people's life movies. In my own life, I've played the role of daughter, mother, wife, colleague, friend, model, motivator, and probably some I wasn't even aware of because we can never truly know the influences we have on everyone we meet. You learn the most from relationships—marriage, parenting, friendship—but this doesn't belittle the impact you have on the many people you interact with casually on a day-to-day basis. It could be that the smile you gave someone on the street turned his mood around for the rest of the day. A simple, effective gesture of kindness goes a long way.

Parenthood is easily one of the roles that has the most influence on your life, and your childhood had the same impact on your parents in ways you can never fully understand. The responsibility of shaping the lives of six children from the time I was barely out of school myself to well into adulthood was my most rewarding experience. Throughout their lives, I've learned just as much from them as they have from me.

Motherhood was my priority as a young adult, and while I did not pursue modeling then, the reasons didn't relate to my role as a parent. Using hindsight, I know that being a model in my sixties has proven to be much more rewarding than if I had done it in my twenties. If anything, it gives Wally the bragging rights of saying he sleeps with a model—much more impressive at this age.

Take a moment and make a list of all of the supporting roles you play in other people's lives. How do you influence them? How do they influence you? Keeping in mind that you star in your own movie and play a supporting role in everyone else's, what do you contribute to make each relationship the most positive one possible?

There have also been times in your life when you've probably influenced, taught, inspired, and encouraged others by example. Maybe someone watched you go through a scene in your life, was inspired, and as a result took action to change her own life. Naturally, other people's actions and outcomes will always be different than your own. The more you recognize this, the better you can be at playing a supporting role and influencing others positively. (See Chapter 16 to delve further into these roles.)

When my second career took off and this book was being written, my children shared in my epiphany that the reality of my childhood starkly contrasted with my role as a mother, which I took on at the age of twenty. They were aware of the conditions of my childhood on some level, but they had never put it together with my role as their mother. Intellectually, they were conscious of the fact that my childhood had been entirely different from theirs, that I had been an only child whose parents had divorced when I was four and that I had gone off to boarding school at the age of seven. They knew I had a mother who flew off to South America as she pursued her career, while I was left behind feeling rather alone and insecure. But making the connection between my background and being the mother of six wasn't something that was apparent to them.

Since we often view our parents as parents first and people second, it's uncommon for children (until they reach adulthood) to see their parents in other roles. When children reach the age at which they can make this distinction, it awakens them and allows them to further acknowledge the complexities of life and how everyone has more than one role.

There are many constructive ways to look backward in order to help yourself move forward. You can do some of them on your own and involve your supporting players in others. All of them are easy to incorporate in your daily life.

Read Your Journal

If you've kept journals or diaries over the years, the screenplay of your life may be right there in the drawer of your nightstand. Next time you snuggle down under the comforter to write, take a few minutes (or more) to go back and reflect on past entries. Keeping a journal brings so many benefits, one of which is reflection. With each new experience, your mind stretches and never reverts back to its old shape. By reading former journal entries, you're given a snapshot of your thoughts and actions taken during a particular period in your life. It gives you a new, distanced look at an experience and can show you how your mind has expanded since that event. Some entries might be embarrassing to read in hindsight, and that's actually great. It means you've learned from the past and will likely not repeat the experience if it was something you weren't proud of. The entries that now cause you embarrassment give you perspective on how much you've grown emotionally or at least provide data that will help you work toward your growth. Ask yourself whether, if the same situation were to arise again, you would handle it any differently, knowing what you know now.

Still other entries will make you proud of how you handled a situation, how you treated someone, or even how well someone treated you (because that shows you were loved). These are the events you can pat yourself on the back for and know that somewhere along the way you gained emotional maturity or success through your thoughts, words, or actions.

If your entries come out heavily on the embarrassing or disappointing side, it may be time to consider how you can work with your emotions and actions to improve them. In time you can have pages that are full of back-patter stories. (See Chapter 13 for more information.)

◦◦◦ Get Your Family Involved ◦◦◦

When it comes to family and memories, every family member has a different scenario for the same memory. Years of Christmases, Easters, Hanukkahs, birthdays, anniversaries, graduations, other milestones, and even everyday events will be remembered differently by and evoke different emotions in each person who participated. It's impossible for everyone to have the same screenplay for their life movies. Supporting roles exist in opening presents, eating coffee cake or pancakes for breakfast, or whatever other family traditions took place, but the emotions and memories are all unique to individuals. By listening to everyone's memories, you can gain perspective on how you've played a supporting role in their lives. It's important to understand how you've affected other people, and oftentimes knowing this helps you make choices that allow you to move forward gracefully.

Family reunions are notorious for raising these questions and can result in fond memories or arguments. As discussions develop around the picnic table, keep your respect for others' feelings intact. One event might have been more traumatic for one family member than it was for the rest of you, and letting these feelings out in the open for the first time can lead to healing if it's done in a safe environment. You may often keep your feelings about a scene from your movie bottled up out of fear, shame, blame, or false obligation. This is very stressful and can cause underlying issues that fester and actually ruin family gatherings rather than making them fun, as they should be. Holding reunions and talking about the past are good ways to conjure memories that have been buried and are all part of your movie. You often need to look back in order to resolve or heal the issues and move forward. (See Chapter 17 for more on family relationships.)

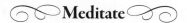

Meditate

Meditation is a venue that provides a safe and wonderful place to explore quietness and reflection. Some people use it simply to quiet their minds and "just be"; others use it for visualization purposes. Either way, spending at least a few minutes a day in a meditative state allows you to reflect. Sometimes I'll be sitting in bed reading a book or working on a project when the urge to simply stop and have a meditative moment grabs me (no, this isn't the same as a "senior moment"). To use meditation as reflection, I almost make a game of it by choosing a time in my life that I want to relive in my mind. With eyes closed, hands and body relaxed, I'll drift into a quiet state and concentrate on a certain time or event from my past. Maybe it's the winter I spent in Havana because the pipes in our New York home froze. Maybe it's the beaches of San Luis Obispo where I spent my summers as a teenager. Or maybe it's attending my youngest daughter Katy's high school graduation—the end of an era. Whether the experience was happy or sorrowful, focusing on it and giving it love for a moment heals or expands it in my mind and subconscious. In meditation I don't spend time thinking about how I could have changed the outcome; that is an activity better suited for journal writing or discussion. I use meditation primarily for simply remembering. (For more on meditation, refer to Chapter 12.)

Keep Track of Your Dreams

Dreaming isn't something you can control, and recording your dreams falls under keeping a journal, but it still deserves a section of its own. The idea of keeping a journal or pad of paper next to your bed to jot down your dreams as soon as you wake up is not new. Certainly there are times when you wake up from a vivid dream but aren't really awake enough to write it down, so you fall back to sleep and don't remember it as well when you reawaken. First of all, don't pressure yourself about writing down your dreams. When you are able to, it's worth putting down as much detail as you can. For instance, if the dream involves water, can you remember if it was a lake or a river, an ocean or a stream? Was the water rough, moving, or still? Deep or shallow? Could you actually see yourself in the dream as though you were looking down on yourself, or were you a part of the action? Were other people there? If so, what roles did they play? Did they take on roles you'd expect them to have or those of other people you know?

Considering all of these elements when you log your dreams can help you analyze them later. There are many terrific resources to help you analyze the meaning of the details, events, and people in your dreams, but the main idea here is to be able to look back in your dream log and see how your dreams correlate with the events and feelings you've recorded in your journal. If you had a lot of dreams about rough rivers during an emotionally tough time, that would explain a lot. Did the dreams settle down over time as the situation resolved?

You often can't remember your dreams well enough to use them to look back at your life, but the few snapshots you do capture can provide valuable information that can help you move forward.

⌒⌒ Go Through Your Pictures ⌒⌒

Since images play a strong role in memory, looking back at pictures, videotapes, or DVDs is an obvious way to review the movie of your life. Friends, family, and events in color or black-and-white images are probably stashed in boxes, photo albums, and desk drawers, or on the side of your computer. Every once in a while it's worth pulling them out and flipping through them. You may decide it's time to throw some of them out, while others bring a smile to your face or a tear to your eye (no, I don't mean the prewrinkle ones). If they are loose in a drawer or box, it might be worth weeding through them and putting them in an album. Giving family members an album of old pictures of themselves as birthday gifts can be fun. Putting the photos together in a framed collage makes a good project for a Sunday afternoon.

Every year Wally and I put together a photo collage for each month of the year and have them made into calendars. The kids get a kick out of seeing the pictures each month. Some photos are recent and some older, but the process of collecting and sorting through them gives Wally and me time to reflect on being parents. The calendars, which we give as Christmas presents every year, help to bring the family closer all year long.

Look at Cards and Letters

Tucked away with your photos, you probably have some old letters and greeting cards. Looking through them is similar to looking at your photographs in that it's fun and helps you revisit your past, this time through the written word. Mother's Day cards that your kids made when they were in elementary school may remind you of the pure love they had for you. Maybe a love letter from your spouse when you first met reminds you he was just as crazy about you as you were about him. A note from a friend you helped through a rough time or vice versa brings a feeling of warmth. Each of your treasure boxes of cards and letters reveals the influence you've had in other people's life movies.

✑ Find Your Yearbooks ✑

Besides laughing at the hairdos in the pages of your old year-books, it's worth taking a glance through them once in a while to spark memories of who you were back then and who you wanted to become. Look closely at the clothes you wore—do you remember how you felt wearing them? Were the things you wore reflective of what was in at the time? (Remember poodle skirts and saddle shoes?) Or were your choices more creative and out of the mainstream? This can reflect how you felt inside your own skin. Did the quote under your senior picture come true? Most likely to succeed? Most likely to become an actress? Most likely to change the world? How many people signed your yearbooks, and what did they say? What did your teachers write?

This isn't a popularity contest; it's about recognizing how far you've come and reflecting on unlived dreams you had back then that aren't too late to fulfill. Youth is a time of wide-eyed dreams and expectations. Going back to that state of mind can inspire you to revisit your dreams. How many of your friends are you still in touch with? Consider going to your next reunion. Jim, Heather, and Katy all had reunions at Green-wich Country Day School in Connecticut in October 2006, and they were all amazed to discover what their old classmates were up to. Only occasionally were they doing what people had expected. More interesting, the people who had been best friends hardly ever kept in touch anymore, and with the change in group dynamics, everyone really had the chance to talk to other people and connect on an entirely new level as adults. Youth is a funny time in that you can never predict what plot twists (fate) and influences will change your path.

When the credits roll at the end of your movie, how do you want people to remember it? Did they laugh and cry? Did they leave the theater with memories of different scenes engraved in their minds? Are you proud of the production that left an imprint on the world that can never be erased? We often don't think enough about how our actions affect others because we become so caught up with ourselves. It's okay in some regard because we are all here to learn our own lessons. But when interacting with others, what might seem like a throwaway phrase to you could have a lifelong influence on them—either negatively or positively. Think about kids in middle school and how brutal they can be to one another. The memories of some of the words they exchange can last well into adulthood.

You can never know when one line in your script can carry over into someone else's movie and rewrite his script. I encourage you not to create bad karma! It will find its way back to you when you least expect it and can change your plot in ways you don't want. By spreading happiness and joy in your role as a supporting player in other people's movies, you can in turn make your own movie a blockbuster hit.

Chapter 10

Putting Your Best
Foot Forward—
Even if It's a Size 10

You gain strength, courage, and confidence by every experience in which you really stop to look fear in the face. You must do the thing which you think you cannot do.

—*Eleanor Roosevelt*

"Your den mother has arrived!" That's what I announced to a dressing room filled to the brim with chic, energetic young male and female models. I was in San Francisco for my first runway show, one of the biggest of the holiday season. It was an annual fund-raising luncheon at the magnificent Fairmont Hotel atop Nob Hill. The event benefited the Boys and Girls Club and was well attended. As I arrived and walked into the ballroom set with tables for more than a thousand guests, I took one look at the enormous T-shaped runway and gulped. I was momentarily overcome with a heady mix of both excitement and stage fright as I imagined what the next few hours would be like. Not daring to pause and reflect for too long, I proceeded to make my way backstage. When I stepped behind the curtains, the scene that greeted me was very much like what I had seen in the movies. The models who surrounded me were giggly girls and vibrant young men.

There was an entire team of hair and makeup people at long workstations filled with every beauty necessity you could possibly think of, and beyond these stations were racks upon racks

144

of magnificent designer evening wear and a table of equally dazzling jewelry. The dresses had come from Wilkes Bashford, one of the finest clothing stores for men and women in San Francisco, and because it was the holiday season, the gowns were especially lavish and colorful. No glitz was left behind. We had all been in for fittings earlier in the week, so we knew what to expect and could relax in the certainty that each outfit would fit perfectly. The other models looked in my direction as I laughingly greeted them and immediately welcomed me into their groups. They never seemed to give it a thought that they had just been joined by a model three times their age. We were all there to do a job.

We paraded through hair, makeup, and a rehearsal. Not only did I have four different dresses to wear, but each trip down the runway was choreographed differently. At times we presented in pairs, and other times we went solo. At last the seats filled and the music began. The audience quieted in anticipation, and we lined up behind the curtains for the show. There were directors with headphones communicating back and forth, ready to instruct us as to when it was time to step out on the runway. With my heart in my mouth, I knew that the moment had arrived. If ever there was a time to swallow my nerves and put my best foot forward, this certainly was it.

The music played and out I went. Down the long runway, turn, off to one side of the tee, pause, turn, smile, look over my shoulder, over to the center, pause, turn, then off to the other side of the tee, and finally back up the runway, pausing in the center and again at the end. Step back behind the curtains and breathe a big sigh of relief. Whew, I had done it! The hard part was over and I knew the rest would be a breeze.

I went through several quick changes between runway walks. The dynamic team of hair and wardrobe professionals immediately descended on me and took me under their wing, especially my hair dresser. He was so kind, and each time I came off the runway he greeted me to fix my hair for the next outfit, but mostly he encouraged and supported me. His presence and assistance made a world of difference to me that day.

Through what seemed like a lot of organized chaos, I felt as though we all blended together like hot tea and honey. I wasn't out to prove to the younger models that anyone at any age could do this, only to model for them that aging gracefully is "in." They were warm and welcoming and never questioned my presence. They treated me professionally and respectfully. (Maybe that's a promising sign of the new generation.) My goal that day was to do my personal best. This was the beginning of a new segment of my life, and if I felt great about it and presented myself well on the runway, I knew I could take away that wonderful feeling of enjoyment and success and tap into it whenever I needed a boost of confidence—kind of like putting the feelings in an emotional bank account that I could draw from later. By focusing my thoughts on my passion for having a modeling career, my desire to be there as a representative of my age group, and tying it all into my earlier life's ambitions, I was putting my best foot forward.

As we busily went about the show, I could feel the positive energy mount. Yet it was the audience who astounded me. They were the ones who clearly took notice of my presence. After all, I was the only silver-haired model strutting down the catwalk. At the end of the show my eyes welled up with tears when I looked out at the sea of men and women, the majority of whom were my age, giving me a standing ovation. Later, in the lobby as everyone left the luncheon, the ladies swarmed around me to say how excited and happy they were to see a model they could relate to. It was in that moment that I felt a strong desire to inspire other women my age to follow their dreams, no matter what they were. As the saying goes, that was the first day of the rest of my life.

Appearing on the catwalk in San Francisco served as a natural high for me, a symbol of my many walks through life: from filling and cleaning baby bottles to juggling BlackBerries in the corporate world to becoming a professional model. I didn't expect or anticipate some of the roles I've played in my life, and that's part of the fun. It keeps me wondering what's next and how I'll handle the challenges and rejoice in the rewards. When this book became a reality, this was one chapter that I particularly looked forward to working on because of my strong belief that when you face life with a positive attitude, you are doing yourself and those around you the greatest service possible. While the next step in this journey is yet to come, I know that there are always new and exciting adventures around the corner if you are open to allowing them into your life. Don't be swayed by hurdles that might pop up. Often they are there to test your passion and resilience. Overcoming what appear to be obstacles along the way ties naturally into my theory of putting forth a positive attitude. Even when all six of my children were under the age of nine and home with the chicken pox or flu, taking the attitude that this, too, would pass helped me see the light at the end of the tunnel.

Starting at a very young age, I learned to always take a positive, can-do attitude, both physically and mentally. Putting your best foot forward (even if it's a size ten like mine) means assessing every situation in which you find yourself, looking at the possible challenges you may face, and then determining in advance how you will handle them if they do arise. It means doing your homework, being prepared, and then going forward and over obstacles with a confident and positive spirit.

Exploring Self-Honesty

Can you think of a recent situation from which you walked away feeling proud that you had showed your best self? Or a situation in which you wished you had done a better job of presenting yourself? If you feel you could have handled a specific event better, think about how you can improve the next time something similar occurs.

There is a delicate balance to displaying your best attitude. It's a way of thinking and being, an art that can be developed with awareness and intuition. Whatever my role—be it as a daughter, a mother, a wife, a friend, a business professional, or a model—I foster a positive attitude with everyone I meet. In Chapter 9, I talked about the importance of thinking positively and how having positive, uplifting thoughts can improve your relationships with others. This chapter focuses on taking those thoughts and acting on them to make them a reality.

Overcoming Challenges

There are days when life catches you by surprise, and you aren't always prepared to handle some of the scenarios that present themselves on short notice. Think about some of the challenges you have been confronted with in the past and reflect on how you handled them. Would you act the same way today as you did then? When something happens of which you've had little or no advance warning or when something turns out to be entirely different from the way you imagined it would be, making a quick mental adjustment and adopting an "I can do this" attitude is key to having a successful outcome. Even if you trip up a little along the way, it's your determination to bounce back that counts. People will love you for trying and for being honest about the challenge that's before you. If you tackle it with humor and grace, you can pull off just about anything.

A perfect example is when Miss USA tripped and fell on the stage in Mexico City during the 2007 Miss Universe contest. With all eyes and cameras on her, she immediately got up and, with a broad smile on her face, continued walking cheerfully, smoothly, and gracefully across the stage. The audience loved her for it, and their opinion of her rose a thousand percent. She was real, just like one of them, and she had immediately turned a negative into a positive. Bravo for her!

⚇ Facing Change and the Unknown ⚇

If you're in your fifties, sixties, or seventies, you may have decided to retire or even move to a new location. It's time to open a whole new chapter of your life. It's all so new and there are many challenges ahead. How will you greet this new time and make it fulfilling and exciting?

Here are some potentially challenging situations that might trigger some thought about being the best you can be, regardless of how anxious or insecure you may feel at first:

ə❧ You're invited to a party and find yourself in a room full of strangers.

ə❧ You're asked to speak or give a toast at a large gathering.

ॐ You walk into a classroom on your first day in a brand-
   new course and the materials and expectations seem
   overwhelming.
ॐ You've just received notice that your spouse or partner is
   bringing home six guests for dinner in an hour.
ॐ You're going out on your first date in decades.
ॐ You've been handed a pink slip because your company is
   cutting back and your position has been eliminated.
ॐ You (or a loved one) have just been diagnosed with a
   serious illness.

You may never encounter some of these scenarios. The idea
is to think about how you present yourself in day-to-day situations. Others that you come up with on your own are worth
writing about in your journal and reflecting on later to see if
you have developed trends when it comes to dealing with certain situations that repeat themselves in your life. The more
you reflect on your actions and thoughts and consider how you
can strive to present yourself well, the more people will expect
that behavior from you. It works toward changing unwanted
paradigms into new behaviors and attitudes that reflect and
show a more positive you. You will learn to love yourself for it
(see Chapter 14) and will likely inspire others around you to
rethink their thoughts and actions as well.

Learning from Experience

By the time I landed a position in public relations I had already
mastered presenting myself well. It became a natural part of my
thoughts and actions over the years and made my new career

that much easier to adjust to. Certainly I wondered about the unknown events that lay ahead of me, but I knew I couldn't control the actions of others, only my own reactions to situations as they arose. In fact, my first days on the job proved to be the most trying of all as I was immediately put to the test.

One of my new responsibilities was to manage all of the photo shoots that took place on the property. One of our brand partners, an automobile company, was scheduled to film a commercial that involved a crew of fifty people filming in numerous locations. The shoot would take place over eight days and entailed organizing and moving the crew from one spot to another. Before dawn on my first day of the shoot, I was running along a dark road coated in a light drizzle to meet the crew and tripped on the edge of the pavement, sprawling headfirst on the pavement in a most ungraceful landing. The pain that immediately shot up my foot and ankle told me in no uncertain terms that I had broken something (I had actually broken bones in my foot and sprained my ankle). I oversaw the remainder of the shoot standing to the side on crutches; however, I refused to be daunted. These people were depending on me to carry them through a large shoot, and letting them down wasn't an option. They sent me roses that evening and brought me treats during the rest of the week, and I in turn gave them the best I had to give. We all laughed a lot as we made our way through the demands of the ensuing week, and the end result was a commercial that was captivating and stunning. I had the choice of letting my fall ruin the week and the shoot or making the best of it. Although I was understandably upset, I chose to continue on with a positive outlook.

This was not the only challenge I faced that week. Days before the photo shoot, I had been diagnosed with uterine cancer and was scheduled for a complete hysterectomy as soon as the crew packed up their equipment and returned to Los Angeles. A few days into the shoot, I went to my doctor for a routine preoperative checkup, and he noticed that I had an irregular heartbeat. Declaring that I couldn't proceed with surgery until after I'd been seen by a cardiologist, he set up an appointment for me. The next day I went through some tests and was diagnosed with a rather severe case of cardiomyopathy. It was serious enough to warrant immediate attention after the hysterectomy but not serious enough to preclude it. The photo shoot continued on, and after more than a week's worth of work, it was over and I had to meet all of the other challenges that had just surfaced.

You can't always control the events or situations that happen to you, but you can control how you react to them. Obviously a positive approach and outlook will always outweigh a negative one. Fortunately there was a happy ending to my little saga: my foot and ankle healed, the cancer was cured by surgery, and my heart ticks just like new, thanks to the wonders of modern medicine and an implanted defibrillator. Although that period of my life was trying, I resolved to rise above it all. Much of my ability to do so was a combination of my passionate desire to excel in my newfound career and my innate ambition to handle life's complications with grace. In every situation you face, you have two choices—one of love and one of fear. I chose love. Love for my new career and love of life.

Being Your Best in Any Situation

Almost every profession and life experience brings us in contact with people. Whether we already know them, it's a first meeting, or a chance encounter, how we handle ourselves makes us memorable to other people whether they are consciously aware of it or not. We leave an imprint of ourselves in their subconscious minds from the moment we connect. This is why it's so important to communicate a positive energy through our inner and outer voices when meeting people.

The Eyes Have It

Greeting someone creates the "dance of the eyes." You look into one another's eyes as you meet and talk. You can instinctively identify the other person's emotions through that eye contact, so when greeting someone, focus on sending positive energy out and it will translate through your eyes. Body language specialists tell us time and again that the direction in which people look while they're talking to you says a lot about the situation. Looking warmly at someone transmits positive energy to that person. It's a great start for putting your best self out there.

A Smile Is Universally Accepted as Kindness

Smiling is contagious. It's what you do not only when you're happy, but also when you're trying to cheer someone up. It's a universal gesture that brings light to others. There's a reason why so many commercials and print ads show people with pearly whites. But all the cosmetic dentistry in the world can't make for a beautiful smile if there's no emotion behind it. You radiate youth and warmth when you smile, bring joy to others, and show that you're ready to give your best to the situation.

Body Language Speaks Volumes

I don't profess to be an expert in body language, but the stances and gestures you use to greet people reveal your state of being

and whether or not you are enthusiastic about meeting or
being with them. It is important to remember that different
cultures have different types of body language. But in general,
a firm handshake and direct eye contact tells the person you're
meeting that you are interested. It shows you care, and by caring about people, you're putting your best self forward because
you're showing interest and possibly empathy. You can always
tell the people who love to make new acquaintances because
they light up as they offer their hands or even give a hug,
depending on the situation and relationship, and their warm
greeting exudes enthusiasm.

You interact with people daily, and no doubt there are times you
aren't in the mood to deal with some of them. But if you go out
on a limb and make an effort to be friendly and sociable, you
will often be surprised at how much it actually cheers you up.

Chapter 11

Learn
Something New

K nowledge is like money: to be of value it must circulate, and in circulating it can increase in quantity and, hopefully, in value.

—*Louis L'Amour*

When was the last time you ventured out and learned something new? I don't mean reading the morning paper and learning a bit of trivia or the story behind the headline of a world event. I mean the last time you learned a new skill, craft, or hobby. It used to be that by the time most people reached their thirties and forties, they'd settled into a lifestyle or career that didn't require learning new skill sets. Or they had been so busy raising children that they hadn't taken the time to continue their own growth by consciously learning new crafts or skills. In recent decades, however, technology has boomed at such a rapid pace that we have all been forced to jump on the technotrain or be left behind at the station.

I found this to be true after Wally and I faced an empty nest and moved to California. Once we were settled, I made the decision to start a career. The first thing I did was to sign up for computer classes. I remember walking in the first day and seeing all of those computers lined up in rows around the classroom. That was about fifteen years ago, so you can imagine what the room looked like—clunky desktop modules with even clunkier monitors. But as scary as the first sight of that room was, that basic computer class gave me the confidence and exposure to technology that I needed in order to land an administrative assistant position at Pebble Beach Resorts.

Technology is an easy example to fall back on because we've all had to face it—even if it's simply to send e-mails to family and friends or use a cell phone. There are so many interesting, challenging, and rewarding skills and hobbies to learn, depending on whether you want to take up a second career or just find something new to do on the weekends.

Overcoming Challenging Mind-Sets

For those of us who go through career changes late in the game, there are often challenging mind-sets that we have to move out of the way, step over, or face head-on in order to achieve our goals. Here are some of them:

- Ageism
- Lack of credentials
- Need for an appropriate degree (bachelor's, master's, Ph.D.) or certification
- Reduced salary
- Low self-confidence

This list provides some of the mind-sets and barriers we can come up against when facing change and growth. But they are just that—a mind-set. The less credence you give them, the smaller they become. Let's address how to overcome them to try something new.

Ageism

This one is easy for me to address simply because of my personal experience. I don't think you can argue with the fact that if I can became a model in my sixties, there probably isn't much you can't do if you put your mind to it. We are fortunate that our age group dominates much of the population, and we are therefore able to support each other demographically as we move into new fields and experiences. Many of the people I've worked with are baby boomers themselves and are inspired by my story and those of others like me, because they, too, are making radical changes in their lives. "Sixty is the new forty" is the prevalent catchphrase, and if we're accepted as forty-year-olds, why not take advantage of it?

Of course, sixty is still sixty—but we've totally revamped sixty. It isn't old anymore. Sixty is healthy, strong, sexy, vibrant, involved, curious, active, and seeking to add new dimensions to life. In short, it's better than ever. We have much in common with the forty-year-olds, yet we also have a tremendous advantage over them. We have maturity, life experience, and confidence on our side. These attributes can take us a long way down the road to new successes as long as we get out there and try.

Overcoming the mind-set of ageism when there isn't a support system in place to guide you can be challenging, but remember that it is a mind-set you're facing, not reality. Whether you're pursuing a new career or a hobby, you might raise eyebrows if it's a traditionally youthful field. Don't forget that I entered modeling at the age of sixty-three by my own accord and through my own perseverance. If you find yourself wanting to break into a new area and you don't have the connections and support in place, you'll have to do as I did and take the initiative. Even though a producer "discovered" me (he suggested that I become a model), it was my actions that made it happen. When you take the initiative, you'll have all the credit and pride in the end, which is always great.

Lack of Credentials

I came into the workforce after being a stay-at-home mom for nearly twenty-five years. On the surface, my credentials were changing diapers, making bottles, cooking meals, tying shoes, and everything else involved in raising six children. But on a deeper level, I had the ability to manage, organize, and deal with conflict. Go on any job interview and these three topics will surely come up. Even so, when I arrived in California, I took the basic computer class because I knew I needed it, and it gave me the credentials I needed to land an interview. Once I walked into that interview, the rest was up to me.

Need for an Appropriate Degree

There are cases where a degree is necessary to change careers. For example, my daughter Heather had been an office manager for fifteen years when she decided she wanted to be an English teacher. With only an associate's degree, she needed two more years of school to complete her bachelor's. Nowadays many schools offer degree programs for adults returning to school. She was fortunate to discover such a program at the University of Virginia, near her home in Charlottesville. Within two years, she graduated with a bachelor's degree in interdisciplinary studies with a concentration in English and secondary education. Her course work was dominated by English classes, and she went on to teach high school English for two years before deciding to become a full-time writer. She went back to school at the age of thirty-five and was younger than many of her classmates who were ten or twenty years older. She discovered that not only did earning her degree open doors that were previously closed, but the experience of going back to school later in life was entirely different from the college experience she'd had when she was eighteen. Everyone she interacted with was excited and motivated to be back in school, and many of them had children of their own who were in college at the same time. Degree programs for adults are available both online and in classrooms, depending on the school and the curriculum.

Degrees aren't always required, thank goodness, because some of us don't want to write papers or sit in a classroom ever again. But some exciting careers, such as massage therapy, personal training, interior decorating, and many computer-related fields, require certification. The training programs vary in scope and venue but provide you with the education you need to enter the field. Because they are much more specific than courses for a liberal arts degree, the training is intense, and you come out of the programs thoroughly educated (assuming you've worked hard). These programs are a terrific way to meet people who have the same interests you do and may provide contacts you'll need later. It's a great opportunity to network.

Breaking into Modeling

Because men and women often ask me about modeling and breaking into the industry, I wanted to share some advice and information given by two top agents in the field: Darren Dyck, the regional director for Mode Models in Portland, Oregon, and Jeffrey Hasseler of Look Models in San Francisco, California.

Q. *What is your advice for someone who wants to break into modeling in her fifties or sixties?*

A. Depending on where you live, check around by going online and doing a search for agencies in the area. Check out their websites closely; see if they look legitimate and if they have any sort of name recognition. Also see what they require for new models. A lot of agencies have an open call where they see potential models, and most of them do this about once a week. Have a couple of snapshots taken—nothing professional; you don't need to lay out any sort of money beforehand—outside in natural light with very little makeup on. You can have some mascara and lip gloss, but they want to see how you photograph. Have some close-ups of your face from different angles, some smiling so they can see your teeth, and then a full-length body shot that shows what kind of figure you have and what kind of shape you're in. Once you have the snapshots, be true to yourself and go with your intuition to see if the agency sounds right. When you go into an open call or have an appointment with an agency, they can pretty much tell right away if you'd be a good fit or not.

Lose all preconceived notions about the modeling business. Don't be insecure, because models tend to grow more insecure the older they get.

Q. *How can you tell if the newspaper ads seeking models are legitimate?*

A. For the most part, anytime you see a newspaper ad, you should definitely be very cautious. Some of the bigger agencies will spread their casting net to build their stable of models. In these cases, they hold events in different cities that are sponsored and in conjunction with other events, usually at a mall or specific store. Use common sense. If you see a small ad on the back page of a newspaper that asks you to show up at a hotel room, or they promise to make you a star—be leery.

Q. *Do you recommend modeling schools?*

A. Modeling schools are especially suitable for children if they're used properly to build self-confidence, get them accustomed to being in front of the camera, and allow them to understand how the business works. But models either have "it" or they don't. It's not something you can teach. When models come in off the street, we just know if they'll work well or not. Then after a photo shoot when we get feedback from the photographers and clients, we really know if someone has it or not. Many agents feel that modeling schools are a waste of time and money and that agencies and clients will teach you all you need to know.

Q. *Do you recommend runway, print, or commercials as best for breaking in?*

A. There's no one venue that's better than another. They're three completely different areas, and it all depends on your comfort level. For example, to do runway work you certainly have to fit into a certain size of designer clothes and have the confidence to walk on the catwalk. You need to have a presence to do these shows. Requirements for print and commercial modeling vary depending on the market, work, agency, and area. Again, it all depends on where you're comfortable—in front of a camera posing in different outfits or playing more of a character in television roles. Do it all if you can. The more marketable you are, the more money you will make.

Q. *What's the scoop on the demand for baby boomer models? What is the industry looking for and how much work is there?*

A. The demand for baby boomers is definitely increasing. A lot more of them are living longer; people are more vibrant and healthy at an older age and that's opening up a whole new market for advertising. For print ads, whether for a hotel or any type of industry, the model is going to be representative of the product. They're looking for people who are attractive and to whom the general population can relate.

Anyone who has an inkling that modeling is something she'd like to investigate and see if she's right for should go for it. There is a certain level of maturity and confidence associated with women over forty, and they bring a whole other level to the marketplace that is definitely worth investigating.

Low Self-Confidence

Self-confidence is a term you hear throughout your life. It is a term that defines you differently from one day and one experience to the next. When it comes to public relations, my self-confidence soars. However, when I was first asked to sit on a panel of speakers at San Jose State University, it was questionable. This was my first foray into delivering an inspirational talk before a large gathering of people. Fortunately, once I was onstage it all fell into place, but the drive from Monterey to San Jose was another story.

Self-confidence comes from experience—the experience that only comes with age. As you master challenges, your confidence grows, and by the time you reach your fifties, you've experienced quite a bit. What I found was that by taking a skill I'd already mastered (for example, modeling or parenting) and applying it to a new experience (public speaking), I already had a leg up. I quickly realized that the audience was inspired by my story, and I used my success as a model to connect to the familiar feeling of confidence. I applied this comfortable feeling to my seat on the panel and was able to relax. Talents are transferable. One experience overlaps another at times, and one can borrow from the other. Don't let a lack of self-confidence stop you from doing the things you really want to do.

Seeking New Challenges

Even though you won't find me learning to ski, there are definitely other adventures I'd be willing to try both before and after I retire. Different seasons can inspire you to try new and different challenges, especially depending on where you live.

If you're in the northeast or mountain regions, you might be brave enough to take up skiing in your sixties, or you might opt for cooking classes instead (what better place to be in the winter than in a warm kitchen learning new soup recipes?). Alternatively, spring and summer are great times to join a gardening group or a hiking club. Fall is a wonderful time to join a book club, hunkering down for cool-weather reads; a craft club just in time for the holidays; or a foreign language class so you can visit a country you've always dreamed about. The point is that every season brings new beginnings and fresh opportunities to delve into something new.

The trick to overcoming obstacles is to be connected to your thoughts and actions. Once you overcome the fear of not being able to do something and start taking action toward accomplishing a goal, you see your dreams fall into place.

If it's a new hobby you're interested in learning, do some research online and see if there are local clubs or groups that address it. You can learn a lot from attending these gatherings, and most are informal with little or no pressure to participate. Many local specialty stores have posters or mailings that announce classes and meetings. For example, stores that cater to cyclists may advertise a weekly group ride; a running shop may hold a clinic for beginners; sewing shops are known for their classes and often have newsletters available by e-mail or snail mail; a store specializing in cookware may hold monthly cooking classes with different themes. At the coffee shop where Heather spends a lot of time writing, there is a woman who teaches a class in how to speak Italian, and most of her students are baby boomers who intend to go to Italy. Many fliers decorate the bulletin boards of coffee shops and libraries announcing upcoming classes and special-interest groups.

The opportunities are plentiful once you start to take notice of them.

On the Internet, meetup.com is a wonderful place for finding local groups that cater to just about every hobby you can think of, including hiking, cooking, writing, politics, language, knitting, scrapbooking, yoga, meditation, travel, games, reading, poker, and many more. The site is free to join and easy to use. If there's a group you want to start, you can do that, too. As another option, look into the continuing education programs in your area. Many of them offer short classes in all sorts of different areas for reasonable prices. These are usually well attended and run for a weekend or several weeks depending on the topic.

No matter what new adventure you're considering, take some time and jot down ideas in your journal (see Chapter 13 for more details). You can make lists as you write about what you want to accomplish. Use your journal to organize your plan of action, especially if it is on a large scale such as going back to school. Write down bulleted lists of things you need to take care of before starting—phone calls or e-mails to potential programs, finances that need restructuring, time allotments, and anything else that comes to mind. The idea is to put pen to paper because doing so is like making a contract with yourself to make your dream happen. What you learn along the way will enrich you beyond anything you can possibly imagine.

ᓚ Coming Up with New Ideas ᓒ

Coming up with ideas of new things to try can feel overwhelming, making it easier to put the whole notion aside. I've listed a few suggestions here to help jump-start your thinking.

Start with Some Reading Material

What Should I Do with My Life? by Po Bronson profiles dozens of people who have made changes in their lives, primarily in their careers. While this book is not a self-help book for changing careers, it provides anecdotes as examples and inspiration.

I Don't Know What I Want, But I Know It's Not This: A 12-Step Guide to Finding Gratifying Work by Julie Jansen is a favorite if you're in the midst of a career change and either need assistance in discovering what you want to do or simply need an encouraging nudge.

A handful of books, such as *1,000 Places to See Before You Die: A Traveler's Life List* by Patricia Schultz and *100 Things to Do Before You Die* by Neil Teplica, guide you through events and places to visit. There might be something in one of these books that inspires you to take on a new hobby or adventure. At the very least they can motivate you to experience new places.

Make Your Own List of Things You Want to Do

Clear off the kitchen table and grab a notepad and pen. Once you're settled with a cup of coffee or tea, make a list of hobbies or activities that you used to enjoy and haven't done in a while. If it's easier, go by decades—what did you really enjoy doing in your twenties, thirties, and forties that would still be of interest to you? The answers might surprise you. Did they involve crafts, sports, travel?

Next, consider things you always wanted to do but didn't. The resources may not have been available to you, or your family and career took priority. Revisit those ideas and add them to your list.

Use Television as an Inspiration

Here's where you actually have permission to be a couch potato. Between Home and Garden, Animal Planet, the Travel Channel, National Geographic, and many others, the ideas are almost limitless. These stations have myriad programs that address just about any hobby, and they do a good job for visual learners by providing step-by-step progress right on the screen. If you find a hobby of interest, you can follow up with Internet searches or books for more details.

Don't Go It Alone

Involve your spouse! Surprise him by signing up for a weekend workshop. Lots of the activities are co-ed, and there are many that would appeal to husbands. Home Depot offers many free classes, and who knows what home improvements might come of that? Along the same line, you can take your new carpentry skills and volunteer with Habitat for Humanity for a weekend. It's a wonderful way to give back to communities, and you'll meet interesting people with a joint cause.

Alternatively, find a local studio that offers glass-blowing classes. The arts are therapeutic and fun. Something like glass blowing can be a great creative release but still masculine in tone.

Explore Your Town

Keep an eye out for happenings about town. Pull out your local paper, especially the weeklies that provide events, and circle anything that looks interesting. Run the ideas by your spouse or a friend and make a date. Also pause and read the fliers on bulletin boards in locals stores, schools, commuter stations, and so on. Something might catch your attention.

Finding new interests and revisiting old ones rejuvenates the spirit. Taking on new challenges helps you feel young and keep your mind sharp. Hobbies you packed away might have been stored temporarily or for a long while, but like all treasures, they are worth rediscovering. Whether you go it alone, with your spouse, or with a friend, trying something new enriches your life and adds a dimension of happiness and excitement to your daily routine.

Chapter 12

Visualization Techniques to Create Your Life

Y ou must see your goals clearly and specifically before you can set out for them. Hold them in your mind until they become second nature.

—Les Brown, motivational speaker

In May 2007, Werner Berger scaled Mount Everest at sixty-nine years young. During his interview with Matt Lauer on the "Today Show" just days after his accomplishment, Berger attributed the success of his climb to visualization. He clearly described aspects of the mental picture he captured of himself at the summit prior to the climb. At the time, he was considered the oldest North American to have succeeded in making it to Everest's summit and was believed to be the fourth oldest person in the world to do so. Berger is a wonderful example of a man who has aged gracefully. Not to mention that when he appeared on the "Today Show," he was engaged to be married. The two lovebirds sat side by side and proudly, yet with great humility, shared their story with Lauer. They are a couple who live and breathe excitement and love.

Berger's use of visualization is a common technique among professional athletes around the globe. Basketball players see the ball swishing through the net before it's released from their hands. Gymnasts visualize themselves midbackflip while they're lying in bed the night before a meet. Triathletes see each arm stroke, pedal rotation, and running step on the course during training sessions or in the car driving to the race. They all see and emotionally feel their performance before actually competing. The most successful athletes are often the ones who practice visualization religiously, be it in the shower, driving down the road, eating breakfast, or lying in bed before dawn. They know firsthand the influences of the strong connection between mind and body. Werner Berger is a fine example not only because of his age, but because he overcame a mountainous obstacle both literally and figuratively.

What You Can Accomplish

Visualization techniques are a critical part of manifesting good experiences in your life, and when you use them in tandem with journal writing (addressed in Chapter 13), you'll be unstoppable. Because both the written word and images are visible to the naked eye, they fall under the category of conscious techniques that impact your subconscious mind. Your subconscious mind stores your unborn dreams.

One of the vision boards that I consciously created as a teen was filled with images of models and the fashion industry. These boards planted the seeds in my subconscious that allowed the garden of a modeling career to grow in my later years. Reflecting on the way my life has unfolded, I'm glad that the dreams I envisioned back then waited to come to fruition until my sixties. For one thing, it afforded me the opportunity to fulfill another dream I had while growing up—that of becoming a mom. Having gone off to boarding school at the tender age of seven, I used to lie in bed at night and imagine what it must be like to live at home with a mother and father who were always there for me. I would read about big, happy families and visualize myself having one of my own. My childhood was often uncertain and lonely, and I longed for normalcy. I wished for a house filled with love and laughter. I'd see myself flipping hamburgers and baking cookies in a sun-filled kitchen with a loving husband and children all around me and a baby on my hip. I knew that was what I wanted someday.

Wally and I agree that we're glad we raised our large family when we did. I'd given birth to all six of them by the time I was thirty. We were young and fortunate to be able to devote ample time and energy to being good parents. Raising a houseful of happy, healthy children in a nourishing environment is by far the most important accomplishment of our lives. Jackie Kennedy once said, "If you don't do a good job raising your children, nothing else you do matters." She was so right.

While the typical progression of life may play out with a woman going from modeling to business career to parenthood, I chose a different road. But along the way I had these three entirely separate visions in my head. Some I knew I would find a way to bring about, whereas the modeling came as a complete surprise. When it came to modeling, the effort and emotion I put into making those early vision boards were key to the process. I took the time to flip through the magazines, cut out the images, paste them on the boards, and imagine what that lifestyle would be like. Seeing these boards on my wall day in and day out, along with my inner passion for the industry, led to the outcome I'm now experiencing. The emotional satisfaction behind the work that went into them was paramount.

As for the timing of the fruition of our dreams, the universe knows when the time is right for dreams to become reality. By allowing fate to take care of the details such as when and how, you are likely to be pleasantly surprised when the time comes, especially if you're sixty-three.

Dr. Wayne Dyer tells his audiences, "If you change the way you look at things, the things you look at change." This is particularly relevant to visualization because of his emphasis on the word *look*. Because you think in images, your individual thoughts are formulated as snapshots. If I ask you to think about your dog, a picture of Fido or Scruffy will probably appear in your mind. Think about your children and undoubtedly images of them (at any stage of their lives) will pop into your head without conscious consideration. Your husband? Yep, there he is in full color on your mental screen. It's simply the way your mind works. This is why visualization is such a powerful tool for creating the next phase of your life.

Remind yourself to look to your future by keeping your eye on what you want to create while living and loving in the present. As I'm moving through one stage of my life, I'm also starting to visualize how I want to shape the next stage or the one after that. Ultimately, your thoughts become reality when they're tied to strong emotions and action. For example, when my children were younger, I thought about what I wanted to do with my life when they were grown and out of the nest. I knew I wanted something that would take me out into the world, a career that would challenge and fulfill me, that would put me in touch with all sorts of interesting new people. I desired new opportunities and a new environment, and I also wanted to be surrounded with glamour, excitement, and fun. I reminded myself that I had grown up with a mother who was far ahead of her time and how inspirational she was to me. She had an adventurous, glamorous career scouting new locations for Intercontinental Hotels; it provided her the luxury and experience of frequently flying off to Brazil and Argentina, as she capitalized on her South American upbringing. Although her lifestyle had its downside for me in the form of time left alone and the insecurities that resulted, her career also opened my eyes to the world of opportunities that were out there for women. Granted, in those days they were not talked about or considered the norm, but I grew up knowing they were there and that someday I wanted to experience them, too—but not until I had fulfilled my first dream of having a large, happy family.

Having these thoughts and images in my mind while living in the moment of cooking dinner for eight (a nightly routine), changing the beds, or taking the children to the pool or skating rink gave me the opportunity to tap into my inner self and explore my future. Sure enough, when they were all out of the house and Wally and I had moved to California, all that I had envisioned over the years started to come true. By then I was in my early fifties, and it was time to make the next stage of the life I had envisioned become a reality. Entering the job market at that age was, of course, a little frightening, but I had a clear picture in my mind and had written so much about it in my journal, that in many ways it was already familiar territory for me. With my eye on my goal, I took baby steps toward creating the next phase of my life and gradually had the satisfaction of seeing it unfold. Over time I went from selling golf balls in the pro shop to learning how to use a computer so that I could become an administrative assistant in marketing; I then ultimately moved into my current position of handling public and media relations for the entire resort. Sometimes I wrote in my journal, sometimes I visualized my next stage, but I always kept my dreams alive through thoughts, emotions, visions, and—when the time was right—action.

Some people are art-shy. The beauty of a journal, vision boards, and meditation is that no one but you needs to know what goes on the paper or appears in your mind. They create a private place that you can choose never to expose.

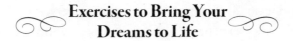

Exercises to Bring Your Dreams to Life

The beauty of visualization is that there are lots of techniques ranging from vision boards to meditation. For example, you can take different approaches and have plenty of room to play with vision boards, or collages, like the ones I made in boarding school. Another option is visualization meditation, which involves mentally seeing and concentrating on your dreams and the experiences you desire. By taking time out every day to visualize both the emotional and physical experiences you want to create, you are using your conscious mind to tap into the wonders of your subconscious.

Basic Visualization Exercise

When you can find a quiet moment in your day to stop and visualize your goals and dreams, you are actually setting the stage for the results in your subconscious. Sometimes the best time to do this is just before you go to sleep or when you first wake up and are still in that half-awake mode. With your eyes closed, conjure up an image of you achieving a specific goal. Involve all of your senses and consider the following:

ঌ Who (if anyone) is with you?
ঌ What are your surroundings like?
ঌ How does it feel to relish your success?
ঌ What scent or sound accentuates the event?

Stay in the moment for as long as you can, and feel your spirit soar as you reach your accomplishment. Take a deep breath and pull it all together. Feel it in the core of your being. Now send it out and surrender it to the universe.

This works as a brief activity and is a wonderful way to begin or end your day. If you do this before sleeping, think about the delightful dreams that are possible once you doze off. Then when you wake up, try it again and notice how your day starts off that much brighter. It's a habit worth creating!

Vision Boards

Art in all its various forms is a wonderful outlet that allows you to focus intently on something other than your day-to-day life. It allows you to escape to a world of desires, which have the potential to turn into reality. Making a vision board is one form of art that anyone can do, even the artistically challenged. Here are the supplies you need:

ঌ A stack of magazines geared toward your desired lifestyle and interests
ঌ Scissors
ঌ Glue or paste
ঌ An art board

ε➤ Colorful pens or markers (perhaps from your kids or grandchildren)

ε➤ Background music to lift your spirits

Creating a vision board is a fun way to spend a rainy afternoon or quiet evening. Flip through the magazines and look for images or phrases that catch your attention. Look for pictures that trigger a positive emotion or reflect the life you want for yourself. Maybe it's a house that resembles your dream home, a beach scene that identifies a new vacation spot, a piece of furniture you'd love to have in your living room—anything that strikes you. Cut them out and put them aside. You can wait to arrange them on the board until you've finished your cuttings, or you can have at it and start pasting from the get-go—whatever process makes you feel productive, engaged, and energized.

Colorful art boards are easy to come by in any shop that sells art supplies. You can choose from several colors or even white; pick a color that makes you feel good. Use pens or markers in different colors to write personalized notes and phrases next to your pictures; this enhances the images and further ties your emotions to the project. For instance, next to a beach scene, you could jot down in red, "Don't forget sunscreen!" The idea is to allow the project to blossom in all sorts of directions and to absorb your body, mind, and soul in moments of pure creation.

You may prefer to dedicate different boards to different themes, such as lifestyle, career, relationships, and vacations. This can help you focus on a specific area of your life that needs a lift. If you're happy in your relationships but want to change careers, creating a career vision board might help push you to the next level. Haven't been on a vacation in a while but know you want to go? Pick up a few travel magazines and thumb through them in search of your ideal paradise. Beach scenes galore—what a beautiful board that would make. Or maybe Europe is your desired destination; the Eiffel Tower surrounded by European landscape and architecture might be your visual ticket that precedes the literal one. Heather created one board for lifestyle that has images of houses, furniture, and vacation spots and one for her writing career that has inspiring phrases related to writers and images of writers' retreats. Many of the images for the latter came from magazines like *Writer's Digest*.

Meditation

Like art, meditation doesn't have to be as daunting as it may seem. There are all sorts of scenarios for where, when, and how to meditate, and plenty of books and CDs teach a variety of meditation techniques. The ones I'm suggesting here are simple to understand and do, but I encourage you to research the topic further to find a method that works best for you.

You'll want to be in a quiet setting and a comfortable position. Whether you use a pillow or mat or sit in a chair, on your bed, or on the floor, make sure you're comfortable, so you will be able to concentrate on meditating rather than worrying about your foot falling asleep. Add to the atmosphere by lighting a candle and turning off the lights. Candles are very relaxing and come in many magnificent scents. If you want, use a candle flame as a focal point to aid your concentration. If you're an outdoor enthusiast, nature provides wonderful places to meditate if you can find a quiet spot. A blanket or bench in a park or your garden, the beach at sunset or sunrise, a big rock alongside a river—anywhere that connects you to nature and beauty is fine. The more peaceful and aesthetically pleasing it is, the better.

Meditation does for the mind and soul what exercise does for the body. A combination of meditation and exercise in your routine provides a balanced approach to life. Taking a few quiet moments to clear your head, visualize your future, and escape your past and present invites new energy into your being. You'll flush out old negative energy and replace it with a revitalized outlook on life. Just like a massage at the spa or a bubble bath at home, you'll feel better inside and out for having taken the time to escape.

Using meditation with visualization is a process of creation rather than an attempt to completely quiet your mind. Once you're settled in and comfortable, allow your mind to float to your dreams. Maybe you knew going into the meditation what you wanted to concentrate on, or maybe your mind will be your guide. Allow the images to flow freely.

There are many possibilities for visualization meditation; the idea is to focus on the outcome of a desire. Do you want to manifest a trip to the mountains to visit friends? Concentrate on hiking the trails, taking pictures of the lush scenery, smelling the fresh mountain air, and enjoying the company of your friends. Planning a surprise birthday party for your spouse that seems overwhelming? See the invitations going out without a hitch, everyone showing up on time with prepared food, the decorations in place, the presents piled up on the coffee table, and the cake in the refrigerator. Everyone is laughing and having a good time, and your spouse is surprised and pleased with the effort you've put forth.

If a negative or undermining thought crosses your mind, pack it up and send it away, and then think the opposite.

For example, if the thought that your sister is habitually late crops up in your visualization of the surprise party, delete it and replace it with the belief that she'll be on time because she knows how important it is to you. The idea is to relax and relish your vision.

The best way to visualize yourself taking action and living in the moment of creation is not to watch yourself doing it, but to imagine that you *are* doing it. As James Arthur Ray describes in many of his books and CDs, visualizing yourself in the process of doing what you desire is the best way to approach this type of meditation. He says to imagine the action through your eyes rather than through those of an outsider looking down on it.

The more details you add to your vision, the better. For example, if you want to make a career change to teaching, you would see the scene through the eyes of a teacher looking out at your students or writing on the chalkboard. Rather than watching the scene unfold from a bird's-eye view, which is fairly impersonal, you're looking through your own eyes, which makes it much more potent.

Just like the athletes who imagine themselves on the court, field, or track, if I were to meditate on my next runway show, I'd immerse myself in the vision of the audience through my point of view from the stage. I'd be looking down the catwalk, putting my arms through the sleeves of the clothes, and even smelling the aroma of hair products in the air backstage. The more senses you can enlist, the more real the meditation will be.

Another easy meditation to do is to visualize everything you want lined up at your door. Imagine each notion being delivered and all you have to do is open the door. The idea is to make what seems intangible appear at your doorstep. Use this meditation as a method to create excitement and energy for your idea. Imagining everything you want lined up at your doorstep is empowering. Later, it would be worth drawing it or writing about it in your journal.

I've spent a lot of time on visualization and will do the same with a personal journal in the next chapter because I believe these methods are not only enjoyable, relaxing, and productive, but they also help to set the foundation for creating desired outcomes in your life. The combination of seeing, believing, and acting on your goals works. Everyone has their own preferences for specific methods, and these tools are used by successful people who learned them in order to accomplish goals. Find your comfort level and make them a part of your routine. As you begin to see results, you will want to use them even more frequently. It becomes a progression that once begun, you won't want to stop.

Chapter 13

Using Your Journal Throughout Your Life

Dreams are . . . illustrations from the book your soul is writing about you.

—*Marsha Norman, author*

When you think of keeping a journal or diary, you probably imagine a teenage girl lying across her bed and venting the frustrations and elations of her latest crush, what party she did or didn't get invited to, who her best friends are, and what she wants to wear to the senior prom. Nowadays, however, journal writing has taken on a powerful new role in women's lives. Oprah Winfrey's popular "gratitude journal" has spawned an extraordinary amount of enthusiastic new journalists. It's refreshing to see so many women out there writing about what they're grateful for and reflecting on the wonderful events in their lives. As someone who has kept a journal her entire life, I couldn't be happier.

I've always seen my journal as a forum, a private place where I can safely express my inner thoughts, both positive and negative. I believe you should regard your journal as a venue for creating the life you want to live, an informal documentary of your dreams, reflections, hopes, and aspirations. While it might be an ideal way to vent frustrations—and it's often better to vent everyday anger in your journal than to take it out on your unsuspecting husband or friends—its real value is the way it makes you think about your life in positive terms and helps you create a more positive future for yourself.

Why Should You Keep a Journal?

I remember when I was a senior in high school and at the age when we all want to be pretty, if not downright beautiful. Part of my journal consisted of a collage of photos showing gorgeous models in fashionable clothes cut from the pages of *Harper's Bazaar*, *Vogue*, *Glamour*, and *Seventeen*. I would stare at these photographs for hours and dream of being like those models, of looking like them someday. I would write page after page about how wonderful it would be to be gorgeous and to have somebody want to take my picture. At the time though, I was a tall, gawky teenager and considered myself anything but beautiful. I was obsessed with writing and dreaming about becoming a model—little did I know then that the dream would come true more than forty years later.

Another dream that I used to write about in my journals was to have a strong, happy marriage and family life. Having grown up in boarding schools, my idea of the perfect life was similar to that of my children's favorite show, "The Brady Bunch," spotted with Norman Rockwell Thanksgiving gatherings; these scenes floated through my head and into my journal. When I was young, movies and television shows that centered on the family theme were my favorites. I was reaching out to fill a void in my life, and I knew that I could someday create that reality; someday I would live in a home with a husband who loved me and children who adored me, whom I would lavish love on in return.

This isn't to say that my early life was miserable. I was very happy in boarding school, and weekends at home in New York City with my mother and warm and fuzzy Italian stepfather were idyllic—cozy, loving, and fun. But I dreamed of having these things every day, not just on occasional weekends. Sunday afternoons when I would go down to Grand Central Station to catch the train back to school were sad and difficult. My journal became my friend and companion on those train rides. I missed my mother and stepfather a lot, which wasn't always considered "cool" as a teenager, and writing in my journal simulated writing a private letter to them. I felt that they would somehow hear my message on a spiritual level. Those entries always made me feel connected to them.

While I dreamed of a large, happy family, somehow I also had a second dream—another vision of what would come after that when the kids were grown and gone. I'm sure I was greatly influenced by my mother and her exciting life in the business world, and I wanted that for myself as well.

When I married and became a mom, my Brady Bunch vision became a reality pretty quickly, and by the time I was thirty I had a strong, happy marriage; a devoted husband; and six beautiful children. My journal writing (squeezed in when the kids were napping or in school or at odd times during the day when I could steal a few minutes) turned to how I could instill in my children all the family values that my husband and I considered important. I wanted so many things for them as individuals and as a group. I wanted them to love each other and be each other's best friends. Of course, that was completely unrealistic. Kids will be kids, and sibling rivalry existed in our household as much as in anyone else's, but I wanted the good things to prevail.

Staying focused on my inner self with six kids pulling on my proverbial apron strings was tough. I struggled to have balance in my life and not give up on my personal dreams. I thought about what my life would be like after they were grown. I looked forward to what would be "my time" and planned to make the most of it. Along the way I jotted down things that appealed to me and creative ideas I had. In doing so, I learned more about what interested me. For example, I realized I liked interior design, so I attended courses at a local community college and then took a part-time job with a design firm when the children were all in school.

How Should You Begin?

Opening a journal to a blank page creates so many possibilities. Putting thoughts to paper is the equivalent of releasing them from your conscious mind, which allows you to move on to the next task at hand, whether it's grocery shopping or cooking dinner.

If you are intimidated by a blank page, try writing down one of the following first:

- Three good things that occurred today (even the littlest things count)
- Three affirmations ("I am loved," "I am healthy," and so on)
- Three things you're grateful for (all of your children being healthy, having a close family, and so on)

None of them need to be more than a short sentence, and you can repeat the same thoughts day after day. The idea is that you will feel grounded and thankful after writing and again when you go back and reflect on your entries. To truly benefit from your writing, you should try to flesh out your thoughts as much as possible, but everyone is different, so don't feel pressured to write a certain amount. You may start out with a few lines and eventually build up to full paragraphs after a time, or you may always keep it short. It is the act of writing that counts; expressing yourself creatively is a healthy way of staying in touch with the things that matter most to you.

Allow for Regular Writing Times

Find a time in your schedule that works well for you, and try to stick to this time every day. Keep your journal handy; I know people who leave theirs in their glove box if they know they'll be sitting in a doctor's office or may have time during their lunch break. As much as possible, try to control interruptions during this time so that you can truly focus on the words you're writing.

Of course, there will be times when keeping a journal simply isn't your top priority or you can't fit it in, and that's okay. When you return to it, you'll be reminded of what a healthy mental release it is and how important it can be in organizing your thoughts, feelings, and plans.

Give Yourself an Inviting Writing Environment

If you need quiet space, find a time when you can write without noise and interruption. If the hum of the world around you is soothing rather than distracting, plan to write while other people are engaged in their own work and not looking over your shoulder. At home, find a corner with big, fluffy pillows and set-tle in with your favorite pen. Just before bedtime is a great time to write; it helps to empty your thoughts onto paper so they're not spinning around in your head when you try to sleep.

Develop a Centering Ritual

Associating journal writing with another pleasurable habit can strengthen your routine and create an atmosphere of self-nurturing. When you are ready to write, consider pour-ing yourself a cup of tea or coffee and having a few cookies to nibble on. Play relaxing music. Take a moment for meditation, deep breathing, or prayer before or after writing down your thoughts, goals, and dreams.

Prompt Your Writing with a Routine Self-Reflection Question

Develop one or more triggers such as "What am I feeling right now?" or "What's on my mind?" that you ask yourself at the beginning of each writing session. One suggestion from author Anais Nin: "What feels vivid, warm, or near to you at the moment?"

Focus on the Positive

It is said that a thought lasting more than seventeen seconds is more readily ingrained in your subconscious, which is a good reason to keep your entries and thoughts positive. Jour-nal writing gives you the option of choosing what to write based on two possible perspectives: positive and negative. The words you pen are a reflection of your thoughts, desires, and soul. Putting a thought from your conscious mind on paper transfers that thought to your subconscious. Therefore, if your journal entries tend to be positive, it follows that your life and thoughts will also be positive. Remember that what you put on paper has the potential of to be created.

Journal Because You Love It

Look forward to your journaling time. When it feels like an obligation or chore, you won't enjoy as many of the benefits. If you think about it as talking to a friend who will never divulge your secrets, you'll warm up to it. Remember not to demand more of yourself than you can give. If you miss one day or several, accept that journal writing, like life, is imperfect and go on. Write the next time you have a chance and always be proud of your accomplishments when you jot them down.

It's fun to buy new journals that fit your personality. A large selection is available in stationery and card shops as well as bookstores, or you can make your own by covering a plain hardcover book with fabric and all types of decorations. Just like your home, make it somewhere that's inviting and warm so that you'll want to return as often as you can.

Create a Positive Feedback Loop

As you continue to use your journal to learn about yourself, you will find that the practice gains a momentum all its own. Discovering your own hidden depths piques your curiosity and stimulates you to continue, setting up a positive feedback loop between your conscious and unconscious mind.

Emphasize Process Rather than Product

An important part of journal writing is simply expressing and recording your thoughts and feelings. Concentrate on the process of writing, maintaining the flow of words rather than worrying about the result. If your goal is to have specific audiences read your piece, go back and edit it later. You can use your journal as the raw material for more polished writing, if you wish.

Learn from Your Own Experiences

It is always good to reread your entries a month or more down the road as your life plays out. Your entries demonstrate your personal growth, which provides a nice pat on the back. Look for patterns and correlations that you can work with or be proud of accomplishing. What's improved? What has stayed the same? Learning from your journal entries is much gentler on your self-esteem than many other processes. Try to be objective when reviewing your life from your current perspective.

Being a true Libra, certain things are central to my core identity: a love and appreciation of beautiful things, healthy relationships, and a balanced life. When my children were young, these things were my main priorities. They were what I focused on and wrote about. Now that I'm living the next phase of my life, the things I used to envision are even more important. My relationships with my husband, children, grandchildren, friends, and colleagues are all of paramount importance to me and enrich my life beyond words. I read inspirational books of all types, and record in my journal the ideas that strike a chord with me. I've found that keeping a journal is a creative way to add balance to my life through all its phases. I still think of it as a road map to the best future I can achieve.

Reflecting on what I've written weeks, months, and years later allows me to follow my growth as a woman. Looking back at my teenage insecurities, triumphs, and sometimes just silly thoughts reminds me that we're all human and life truly is a series of ups and downs that we manage to get through despite our fears to the contrary.

Chapter 14

Loving Yourself

A man cannot be comfortable without his own approval.

—*Mark Twain*

Of all the dimensions of aging gracefully, loving yourself is the most important. Without it, everything else falls by the wayside. There is a simple philosophy that says when you love yourself, you allow others to love you, too. This is simple in theory but often difficult for some people to achieve. Like anything in life that seems daunting, taking small steps is a good way to start. If your supply of self-love is running low, think about (and even jot down) the little things you do that demonstrate self-love, and before you know it, your supply will soon feel replenished.

When you make a commitment to working out and eating well, you're loving yourself. When you challenge yourself to learn something new, you're loving yourself. When you take the time to put yourself together, such as choosing clothes in styles and colors that flatter you, finding a haircut that frames your face just right, you're loving yourself. When you choose positive thoughts and actions in interactions with friends, family, colleagues, and even the bank teller, you're loving yourself. When you make the time to write down your dreams in a journal or create a vision board, you're loving yourself. When you develop friendships and other relationships that encourage your happiness, spiritual health, and growth, you're certainly loving yourself. By paying attention to and working with these aspects of your life, you're showing others that you respect yourself and, most importantly, you're expressing self-love.

Keep in mind that self-love is not about ego. Rather, it is a reflection of your inner emotions and how that energy radiates outward to show others who you are and to embrace them as well. When you take time to grow as a human being, all three of your dimensions—body, mind, and soul—have the ability to flourish. Feeling good about every aspect of who you are makes it easier to love yourself, and by keeping your thoughts and actions positive and your energy high, you will feel good about being you.

Because of the way I've lived my life, I've learned that you can only give others the amount of love you have for yourself. Love doesn't work like a credit card; you can't give something you don't have and then pay it back with interest later. It is more like a personal savings account; something has to be there before you can make a withdrawal. Love comes from the heart, and if your heart is filled with self-love, then you have enough to give friends, lovers, spouses, and children. Everyone benefits from you loving who you are. If your savings account of self-love is low, however, you limit the amount you can give to others.

Showing others that you love and enjoy being who you are can be infectious. Walking into a room when you radi-ate self-love turns people's heads—they take notice and feel your entrance before they even look up. They also tend to look inward and ask, "Do I possess that energy?" It's human nature. The idea is not to make anyone feel inferior, but to inspire them to improve their own self-love. For example, when I go to New

Self-Love in a Box

- Smile at yourself when you look in the mirror.
- When someone compliments you, thank them and believe what they say.
- Make a list of your wonderful qualities and stick it on your mirror to read while you brush your teeth.
- Give yourself a time-out when you're feeling overwhelmed. Count to ten or take a few deep breaths.
- Take quiet time for yourself during the day to reflect and renew.
- Celebrate your milestones and accomplishments with friends and loved ones, and rejoice in theirs.
- Exercise to build your strength and energy.
- Eat well to raise your stamina and promote good health.
- Leave time in your schedule for your favorite activities.
- Laugh and love often.

York City, I love going places with my friend Laurie Dhue, a Fox News and "Geraldo at Large" correspondent. Her energy is so high that when we walk into a restaurant, people are drawn to us because the two of us exude enough life, love, and laughter to electrify the city. A girls' night out or a lunch date with Laurie, who is about thirty years my junior, always makes me feel young and alive. (See Chapter 16 for more on cultivating enriching friendships with people of all generations.)

Because of my belief in self-love, I made an effort to raise my children to love themselves as well, partly as a role model and partly through encouraging them to do so. Learning self-love requires making a conscious effort, but the benefits are boundless.

Take your own time-out. Parents often give them to their kids, but actually, we can all use a little time-out once in a while. Most children act up when they're tired, hungry, overwhelmed, and frustrated. These traits and emotions don't disappear as an adult. We all encounter these moments; it's how you handle them that matters. There are times when you simply need quiet time to think and regroup from your hectic life. Taking time for yourself is not about being selfish or egotistical. It is about making yourself happy and fulfilled so that you can turn around and make those around you happy, too.

This idea did not come easily to me. Like many moms, I always put my family first, never taking time for myself. With six children and a husband to care for, not to mention numerous household duties, it was easy to put my own needs on the back burner—if not ignore them altogether. It wasn't long, however, until I started to look in the mirror and wonder who this tired-looking woman was and what had become of the person she used to be. Where was the girl with the outside interests and cozy circle of girlfriends? Where was her healthy, toned body; clear skin; and shiny hair?

Then one day when I was standing in the kitchen folding yet another load of laundry, the epiphany came. If I didn't start taking care of myself and doing a few things just for me, how in the world was I going to be the best I could be for my family? That did it. From that moment on, I vowed to go back to my normal custom of dressing well, taking better care of my skin and hair, finding more time to spend time with friends, signing up for a fitness class, taking up at least one old hobby that had previously given me pleasure, and diving back into journal writing.

I did all of these things over time and discovered that if you look your best and fulfill yourself in ways that stretch your mind and open your soul, you feel infinitely better about yourself and your attitude is greatly improved. By looking your best, I don't mean that you have to be dressed up, but you should dress in a manner that is appropriate to your lifestyle. Please, please, please, no baggy sweatpants and sweatshirts! It's amazing what taking five minutes with a little makeup can do. Treat yourself to a good haircut, and take the time to exercise. Believe me, loving yourself enough to take care of your needs will pay off in ways you can't even imagine.

All of these things applied to me when I was a young mom, and they are just as true today, only in a different way. I still know that when I take the time to look my best, I will feel my best, too, and the added confidence it gives me when I head out the door is reflected in my attitude toward others and in theirs toward me. When I feel strong, vibrant, confident, and healthy, that energy radiates out to everyone I come in contact with and even the grayest days are filled with sunshine and light.

Accept Who You Are and Grow

This is sometimes the hardest thing to do, but learning to accept who you are allows you to grow and move forward. Taking a good look at yourself opens the door for change—a big first step! Once you accept your perceived shortcomings, you can look at them for what they are and work on replacing them with more admirable behaviors or traits.

I was pretty shy growing up, and even as a young adult I didn't have half the self-confidence that I do now. Twenty years ago I would have thought that one of the last things I would ever want to do was to get into public relations. The idea of putting myself out there in front of strangers every day, interacting with them, and handling myself with ease and comfort in any number of unfamiliar situations was unthinkable. Still this was a field that I wanted to move into because I could see that once I overcame my initial shyness, I would be good at it. My natural love of people (well, most of them) and the genuine pleasure I take in building relationships would make me good at it. So I persevered, and it wasn't long before my reticence became a thing of the past. Soon I felt myself blossoming into a new and confident person, relating easily to others and feeling completely at ease as I walked into a roomful of strangers.

Forgive Yourself for Past Mistakes

Too often we're stuck dwelling on past mistakes. Stop! Mistakes don't define who you are; they define who you were. Every minute of every day allows you to change that misconception. The saying "A leopard can't change its spots" is only true if you believe it to be true. I know plenty of people who have moved on from past mistakes and learned to forgive themselves and love themselves again. In fact, your soul's journey is to do just that. When you don't learn and accept the lessons you were meant to learn, the same lessons are thrown back at you time and time again until you do learn them. They may wear a different disguise each time, but they're the same. It's your role to understand and move on, not to remain permanently mired in the past. You need to accept mistakes as opportunities to learn and then grow beyond them. Surely other mistakes will follow, but they will be new ones and they won't define you any more than the earlier ones did as long as you learn from them.

Take Time for a Healthy Lifestyle

Part 1 of this book focuses on improving and maintaining your physical health, which helps graceful aging. It's also important because by taking the time to care for yourself physically, you are proving that you love yourself. Besides, the endorphins that kick in during exercise will elevate your mood, the blood flowing to your cheeks will give you a healthy glow, and the well-toned body that results will boost your self-confidence.

Part 2 discusses keeping your mind healthy and positive, and this, too, is part of taking time for yourself. Meditation, visualization, and new interests are all aspects of leading a healthy life. Exercising, eating well, and expanding your mind all open avenues for new dreams and ambitions.

Treat Yourself to Something Fun or Special

Expecting or waiting for others to treat you to something special often leads to disappointment. While it's nice when people surprise you, it's more than okay to indulge yourself along the path of life. If you've recently lost ten pounds, celebrate. If you went back to school to finish a degree, reward yourself. These celebrations and rewards can fall into any category; just treat yourself to something you want. It can be something as simple as a cup of iced coffee and a Girl Scout cookie, or something as elaborate as that piece of jewelry you've always wanted. That's the point. Loving yourself means not feeling guilty when you spoil yourself. While others mean well and their gifts carry sentimental value, some of the gifts you give yourself are the most valuable.

∞Leading by Example∞

Modeling is not about the superficial layer of looking great, but about exuding an inner glow that finds its way to the audience, just like when the television cameras are on my friend Laurie. As a correspondent, she radiates and projects her energy and confidence to her audience every day. But television and modeling don't hold the reins. Teachers are another perfect example of people who project confidence to an audience. They stand in front of their students knowing they are going to fill those young minds with new thoughts, experiences, and lessons. Teachers who radiate excitement about their topics allow students to absorb that energy, and the students who obtain this new knowledge are changed forever. Almost everyone has a teacher whom they identify as their "all-time favorite." In many cases, their lives were affected because a teacher cared when no one else seemed to, which allowed the students to believe in themselves, or the teacher introduced them to something new that stuck with them for life. Growing up in boarding schools under the watchful eyes of teachers and then marrying an educator exposed me to the impact they create in our lives. When my husband finished his forty-five-year teaching career, he received more than one hundred e-mails, letters, and phone calls from former students congratulating him on his retirement and thanking him for the contributions he had made to their lives. By positively affecting other people's lives, we in turn receive great amounts of self-love. In knowing we've made a difference in someone's life, accepting her gratitude, and receiving recognition for it, we discover that giving without expectation and serving others is the greatest gift we can give ourselves.

Learn to Laugh

Being able to laugh often, with others and at yourself, is a significant sign that you have self-love. Share fun stories and listen to others enjoy telling theirs. Laughter is one of the healthiest things in the world, and the ability to laugh at ourselves is healthy indeed. I always try to see the silliness, the ridiculous, the humor in things—and particularly in myself. You can accomplish this by realizing that there is polarity to life and that everything has both a positive and a negative. By looking at the positive, you can often bring laughter to the foreground. If it's genuine and kindhearted, you'll succeed in spreading it.

No matter what stage of life you're in, if you can take the time to love yourself, the rewards are limitless, especially in terms of health, relationships, and service to others. The old saying that "if you're not happy, then no one around you will be happy either" is true. So toss out the guilt and the "I really shouldn'ts" and take the time to invest in and reinvent yourself so that your savings account of love is filled to overflowing. You won't regret it.

Part 3 *The Soul*

Chapter 15

Bringing It
All Together

207

There is one spectacle grander than the sea, that is the sky; there is one spectacle grander than the sky, that is the interior of the soul.

—*Victor Hugo*

When you hear of someone referred to as an "old soul," it conjures up images of an old spirit living in a young body. As adults we marvel at such children when they spout words of wisdom that make us shake our heads and ask, "Just how does he know that?" We've all come in contact with them—children who display empathy, wisdom, and understanding beyond their years.

There are people of all ages who glow with a vibrant spirit. They seem to glide through life as if they were marionettes on tension-free strings. These are the people whose smiles seem permanent. They celebrate life, making it look like an amusement park ride. They live in each moment and cherish their experiences no matter what life sends them. When you ask them how they are, nine out of ten times they respond positively and have a new story to share. You feel better just being around them, and if you hear their laughter in the next room, it puts a smile on your face. These people have the knack for spreading light and joy and making others want to know their secret.

Sadly, there are also people whose spirits are suppressed. They are in constant need of uplifting and feel as though life has branded them as victims. Their bodies and minds suffer from a lack of vitality and zest for life. Conversations with them can drag you down and drain your energy. An effort to put smiles on their faces may be temporarily successful, but they never last. Certainly you, too, have days when you don't want to venture past the front door, when you'd rather curl up in bed with a cup of warm soup and forget about the outside world.

But allowing yourself to live day to day in negativity is denying all of the gifts that life has given you to explore and experience. Not only do you shortchange yourself, but you do a disservice to those around you. It saddens me to see people in despair because I don't think life has to be like that. When your spirit is drained, you transmit an energy to others that demonstrates the saying "Misery loves company." I encourage you not to choose misery.

If you feel that you fall into this category, pay close attention to the suggestions in Chapters 8 and 14 and do what you can to take action to improve your positive thinking and self-love. Remember that what you focus on expands. This applies to all things in life, so if you spend time focusing on the negative, you will continue to draw negative emotions and events into your life, which leaves you in a perpetual state of disconnection.

Mental Health Days

You're entitled to these days, and they can actually be very healing if you use them as part of your work on inner growth and development. A mental health day can do wonders to regenerate your mind. Journal writing, reorganizing a closet, baking brownies, or just allowing yourself to sob through a really sad movie can be extremely therapeutic, and you can go forth and face the following days with a brighter and more productive outlook.

Fighting the Blues

Your body and mind are not connected to your soul when you are in a funk. When the three are disjointed, you feel out of sorts and disconnected. You can reestablish the connection by lifting your spirits and living in the moment. When I feel myself slipping into a low mood, I have a number of different ways of reversing it. One of my favorites is to take my iPod; tune in to some happy, uplifting music; and go down to the beach for a walk. Another way is to get together with a friend and do something that we both enjoy, even if it's just having a cup of coffee. A great way to overcome the blues is to lend a hand to someone in need because helping others takes the focus off you. Rather than mope around in a bad mood, take whatever positive action works for you to move away from it. You will soon be finding much more enjoyment in all that life has to offer.

Everyone succumbs to the blues now and then for any number of reasons. Ups and downs are a part of life. If activities you used to consider fun, like visiting friends or taking a daytrip, no longer bring you joy, there may be a deeper, underlying issue that you ought to explore with a professional. Feelings of depression that last a while without change or much fluctuation can have long-term effects on your emotions. The medical field refers to this as clinical depression, and it's imperative to seek the type of counseling and/or medication that is most appropriate for your condition.

Walter Matthau and Jack Lemmon starred in the two movies *Grumpy Old Men* and *Grumpier Old Men*, playing on the idea that as you age you naturally become grumpy. But growing old doesn't have to mean feeling down in the dumps day in and day out. The problem of depression arises more often than most people realize, and you may need medical help to overcome it. There are many options for combating depression, but unless you seek help, your struggle will probably continue. Depression is often missed or goes untreated in older adults for a variety of reasons. Identifying depression isn't always easy, and it goes beyond plain old grumpiness. Mood swings can confuse diagnoses because the changes may be caused by one or a combination of medications (such as those prescribed for heart disease and arthritis). Look for signs besides being grouchy or gloomy, such as feeling confused or having trouble focusing attention. Sometimes symptoms of Alzheimer's or other diseases actually mask depression.

Finding the right diagnosis and medication to fight depression may take time and requires that you be honest when working with your doctor. Discuss any major life changes with your doctor, such as the death of a spouse, parent, or child (you never think you'll outlive them), because these events have a devastating impact on your emotional well-being. Wally's mother suffered from Alzheimer's disease for several years, and we know firsthand the impact it has on both the patient and the extended family. Watching out for and being there for one another during these times is critical. Reach out for help when you need it, too.

No matter what the cause of your depression may be—taking medication, a major life event, and so on—finding the right diagnosis early makes a world of difference. Some people seek therapy from a licensed social worker, many of whom offer one-on-one counseling and have a different approach than a traditional psychiatrist or psychologist. Other sufferers seek help through a trusted spiritual adviser. Finding what works best for you and what can provide the healthiest outcome is your mission and goal. It's not always easy to diagnose depression, but with the range of medications and traditional and nontraditional measures available, it's more than likely that you can find one that's effective for you.

Aligning the Dimensions of Body, Mind, and Soul

Now that we've discussed the different ways of addressing bad moods and depression, let's look at how the soul connects to the body and mind. When I want to shake things up, get out of a rut, or create new and exciting experiences in my life, I consciously concentrate on aligning my body, mind, and soul. When the three are in alignment, the possibilities for adventure, growth, and excitement are limitless. Many exceptional books and videos by teachers of spirituality discuss creating the life you want by being spiritually connected to what is known as your "source energy." Bob Proctor, James Arthur Ray, Wayne Dyer, and Deepak Chopra are all notable authors. In fact, it was Deepak Chopra who said, "We are not victims of aging, sickness, and death. These are part of the scenery, not the seer, who is immune to any form of change. This seer is the spirit, the expression of eternal being."

His message reminds us that we are part of a large whole, and our physical and mental selves are only a portion of our existence. He is suggesting that aging, sickness, and death come from our point of view, and our view is within our control as the seer. Fortunately, we are able to connect the body and mind to the soul, which is the bigger picture of self. The soul is always knowledgeable beyond the physical years of the form it embodies. Its purpose as the higher self is to guide us through life and to send us messages as to what direction to take and what decisions are right. These messages come in the form of gut feelings, intuition, and dreams. Sometimes I feel that the soul is part of an external essence of ourselves, as though it's an outer layer of our being, possibly because we don't understand its full function in our lives. Other times we know on a deeper level that the soul truly sums up who we are.

Have you ever heard yourself say that something was meant to be? There are times when life unfolds in a way that you would never have anticipated or expected, but you instinctively know that the experience or opportunity presented is exactly right for you—that it is setting you on a path that was destined all along. When you are tuned in to your inner self, that spirit within you that defines who you are, and when you are open to signs from the universe that point you in the direction of

Reconnecting the Body and Mind to the Soul

When you're "in the moment" is often the time when your body and mind are most deeply connected to your soul. The idea is to indulge in an activity that keeps you focused and allows you to live in the moment. Here are some activities to try:

- Practice yoga.
- Meditate.
- Write in a gratitude journal.
- Exercise/take a walk.
- Volunteer.
- Watch an uplifting movie.
- Indulge in your favorite hobby.
- Re-read your favorite novel.
- Work in the garden.

opportunities that are right for you, then the possibilities for expansion are limitless. This is what I mean by connecting the body, mind, and spirit.

You can reach your aspirations through your awareness of self, and when the time comes to see how your dreams are created, it's a remarkable experience. My life in the public eye was apparently inevitable, but until I met David Krieff, president and founder of Destiny Productions, while he was scouting a possible location for one of his television shows, I didn't know how it would happen. He told me that he was struck by my "inner and outer beauty," and that I should go into modeling. I thought it was a Hollywood line that he probably used often, but he proved to be serious when he sent my photos to people in the modeling industry. That was the beginning of my life-altering experience, and each day my development continues as I explore how this concept of body, mind, and soul works.

Chapter 16

Building Friendships
to Feed Your Soul

It is one of the blessings of old friends that you can afford to be stupid with them.

—*Ralph Waldo Emerson*

If you go into a bookstore or surf the Net, you'll find tons of books on relationships; some focus mostly on marriage trouble, some feature advice for singles, and others give advice to parents. But strangely enough, you'd have to delve deeper to find a book that addresses or includes the art of developing and maintaining quality friendships. It's too bad because there is an art to finding and keeping good friends.

We all know that friends have a tendency to come and go. Some stay with you forever, some leave forever, and some drift in and out of your life at different points in time. But the special friendships that are a source of support throughout your life are the ones worth cultivating. You develop different levels of friendships with different people. Some are friends you meet for coffee and chitchat once in a while, and then there are others you talk to and confide in almost daily and who are there for you during life's trials and triumphs. Each kind of friendship is important and can add a great deal to your life.

As valuable as friendships are, they can be hard to come by. For example, it can be tough if you suddenly find yourself in a new place and it's hard to get around to meet new people, or if you're used to socializing with your husband or partner as a couple and suddenly find yourself alone. Additionally, you may find it difficult to approach new people or nurture relationships past the point of acquaintance. Making good friends sometimes isn't easy.

The Importance of Friends

What's more enjoyable than sitting around a table with good friends laughing and having fun? When Wally and I lived in Greenwich, our friends David and Ann Griswold often came over for cards. Many nights were spent indulging in game after game of gin rummy. The kids meandered in and out of the kitchen, but during the summer months they were most likely outside playing with other children and cultivating friendships of their own, while the four of us sat playing cards and talking about everything that came into our minds.

It was during our time in Greenwich that Wally and I formed valuable friendships that have continued into our senior years. Fellow faculty members and their spouses were the crux of our social life. In addition, my own circle of friends evolved through my part-time jobs for an interior decorator and Talbot's clothing store. Believing that positive people attract other positive people, I have always cultivated friendships with those who share my optimistic outlook on life, regardless of their age or what they do for a living. In fact, I make a point of surrounding myself with younger friends and colleagues; I know they help keep me young. Surrounding yourself with diverse people and viewpoints keeps you stimulated, keeps your mind open to new ideas, and may get you to try something you never have before.

While living on the campus of Greenwich Country Day School (GCDS), we were fortunate to have a built-in social network through ties with fellow faculty members. We all took turns hosting parties; we sat for hours doing crossword puzzles with each other by the campus pool on weekends and summer evenings, everyone taking responsibility for watching the kids in the water; and we shared our experiences as faculty living and raising children. There's a certain camaraderie inherent to living on a private school campus. During the 1980s when our children were at peak childhood ages, it was safe for them to be independent and enjoy the eighty-acre campus, which boasted swimming pools, tennis courts, playgrounds, gymnasiums, playing fields, and a nearby skating rink. They could ride their bikes into town or around the neighborhood, and we didn't need to be concerned.

The safe environment naturally did not mean the kids were safe from falls from trees, spills off their bikes, or playground mishaps. In fact, when Heather was eight years old and fell off a slide at the playground, it was another faculty member who heard her screams from across the fields and drove her to the hospital while our daughter Anne ran home to tell me what had happened. By the time I met them at the hospital, the doctors were already setting Heather's arm in a cast. Our neighbor thought nothing of rushing her to medical attention, knowing I'd be close behind.

Given this situation, our work-related friendships were exceptional. Because we all lived and worked within close proximity of one another, our friends really became extended family, and just as in any family, there were occasional drawbacks to this scenario. Each household had its own personal issues to cope with, and living in a fishbowl environment was not without its difficult moments.

Our twenty-eight years at GCDS were where Wally and I cultivated lifelong friendships that helped define who we were and where we are today. The majority of our neighbors have moved to other parts of the country, but we manage to keep in close touch with the help of telephones, the Internet, and visits. We consider the friendships we made there some of our very best.

What I've learned from our experience at GCDS and through the many friends we've made since moving to Pebble Beach is how much friendship adds balance to our social and personal lives. Our children were all athletic, involved students and had good friends of their own. I believe that Wally and I modeled for them what it meant to develop and sustain quality friendships. They were also very close to our friends and were used to associating with and respecting adults. Since Wally and I were both only children, most of our friends became surrogate aunts and uncles.

In our forty-eight years of marriage, Wally and I have been one another's best friends. We consider ourselves very fortunate because we have seen our friends and even our own children go through divorces in which not only a marriage was lost, but a friendship as well. Also devastating is the death of a spouse or family member who was a best friend. The adjustment takes time, and the loneliness can be paralyzing without the help of friends or focused support groups.

Whether they are with family or friends, I want to emphasize that having relationships with people who are both young and old, men and women, is crucial to my personal growth and happiness. Each age group provides a fresh outlook that contributes to a balanced view of life. Many of my friends are young men and women who inspire me and help me keep my thoughts young. I return the favor by being a role model for them as they approach different milestones in their lives. These are the symbiotic relationships that are worth reveling in.

Making Friends

Luckily, meeting people is a bit easier now than it was even just a few years ago. In the past, many mothers were so incredibly busy running households without advantages like microwaves that it was difficult to find the time to get out and socialize. In a time when most neighborhoods were safe for kids to go out and play, mothers stayed home and expected the children to show up on time for dinner. The opportunities to meet other women were limited. Coffee shops as we know them today didn't exist. Other than those in elite society, most families didn't have nannies to lend a helping hand and provide a chance for Mom to go to the gym or shopping, let alone have lunch with friends. The Internet wasn't an available resource for staying connected or finding people with similar interests. Over the years, the dynamics have changed, but the art of finding and developing friendships still remains a challenge for some women, whether they are twenty-five or sixty-five.

As you know from witnessing your parents' generation, as people lose spouses, family members, and friends, loneliness settles in and can deplete their spirits. The losses can come from death, relocation, divorce, or changes such as retirement and empty nest syndrome. Then there are those who never married or had children and now find themselves alone at a time in their lives when they strongly desire and need companionship. The scenarios are numerous, but fortunately the solutions are as well.

How do you go about making new friends? I've suggested places that allow for such opportunities in several chapters of this book. For example, there are the gyms and yoga studios mentioned in Chapter 3; these are prime locations for socializing before and after class. The continuing education classes and book clubs mentioned in Chapter 11 also involve interacting with others and are wonderful places to establish friendships and nourish your social skills.

Start by finding opportunities to connect with people with whom you have similar interests. Websites such as meetup. com provide thousands of listings of groups under such topics as book clubs, language, investing, travel, new-to-town, cooking, hiking, cycling, yoga, meditation, card games, music, weight loss, divorce support, movie enthusiasts, and alternative health. The purpose is twofold; not only do you learn a new skill or find out more about something you're already interested in, but you increase your chances of making new friends. These groups tend to meet at least once a month (often more frequently), and there is something in just about every town and city around the country. It's also easy to join. Some people belong to several groups at once and probably never have a dull weekend. If you don't have access to the Internet at home, try your local library or ask a friend, neighbor, or family member to help you. Once you're done clicking, head out the door to where the action is!

Becoming Internet Savvy

Throughout this book I've suggested using the Internet, yet it's important to note that caution should always be used when utilizing this technology. Do your homework and be careful when interacting with others online. It's a wonderful tool when used with common sense, but if something doesn't feel right, avoid it. Have a friend or relative help you investigate a site if you have any doubt about it. Using the Internet to seek information about where a group is meeting rather than engaging in one-on-one interaction with individuals is a safe bet. Make follow-up phone calls, if possible, and enlist the help of others whom you trust until you feel safe in a specific Internet site.

Connecting with people provides you with so many opportunities to grow emotionally and spiritually. It not only helps you befriend others, but you encourage others to befriend you. Symbiotic friendships are healthy and rewarding. There are times when you're just too busy to invite friendship into your daily life, and you don't realize how much you miss having them until you come up for air and look around for someone to connect with. Work, family, and health issues are just a few reasons that friendships are neglected, and at times not by your own choice. But just as exercise is good for the body and meditation is good for the mind, friendships are good for the soul. Besides, who else can you discuss your family problems with? Family members can be your best friends and support system, but often your friends know an entirely different side of you and can offer a much different perspective. That balance is healthy.

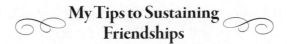

My Tips to Sustaining Friendships

Sustaining friendships takes work but the effort you put into doing so will reward you with support, gratitude, and warm memories along the way. Keeping valuable friends for a lifetime is worth the effort.

Be in It for the Long Haul
It's healthy to keep in touch with both your local and your long-distance friends—through occasional visits, if possible, but certainly by phone and e-mail. They are often your oldest friends, so always let them know how greatly you value their impact on your life. These are the people to whom you will turn in times of crisis, even at a distance, and for whom you will be there in return. Plan times to get together so that weeks and months don't slip by. Schedule time for your friends the way you would anything else that's important in your life. These relationships are among the richest that life has to offer.

Focus on Being a Good Listener
Listen with your whole heart and be "in the moment." Avoid interrupting with your own story about what your friend is telling you. Give her your undivided attention and focus on her. You'll get your turn to talk when the time is right. Remember, people would rather talk than listen.

Empathize

Learn the art of empathy so that you can truly put yourself in your friend's shoes and feel what she is feeling and experiencing. Listen with empathy and offer advice only when asked. Sometimes people, especially women, want to be heard and not advised. When your friend needs a sympathetic ear, step up as someone who will listen. When appropriate, let the professionals give the advice. And for goodness sake, honor and respect your friend's trust in you. If she asks you to keep what she's confiding confidential, *keep it confidential!* Whether it's potential good news that she doesn't want released yet—perhaps she's up for a position at a better company—or bad news such as a pending divorce or a health issue, if she believes her secret is safe with you, don't risk a solid friendship by gossiping. That's the fastest way to lose friends, and as you know, they're not always easy to replace.

When I first started modeling, the agencies put my name in for some pretty big gigs and I was anxious to tell people about them, but I soon learned to tell only my close friends or else the rumors would fly that I already had the job. It left me with a lot of backtracking and explaining to do. This isn't a position you want to be in. Confide in the people you trust and return the favor when they confide in you.

Provide Nonjudgmental Support

A friendship should provide a safe haven to share intimacies without the fear of judgment or condescension. This works both ways. Both of you ought to feel comfortable and be able to take solace in opening up.

Be Willing to Share Yourself with Others

By letting your friend see beneath the surface to the real you, you help deepen that friendship. This will help keep the relationship from becoming superficial.

Show Your Gratitude

When a friend goes out of her way for you, be thoughtful by showing your gratitude. Send little unexpected cards, small gifts, notes, and things to let your friends know that you are thinking of them and appreciate having them in your life.

Know That Friendships Are as Important as Other Relationships

Not only do friends enrich your life, but they are often the glue that sustains you through the difficult times. Established friendships are more important than casual relationships because your friends will support you when the casual acquaintances have come and gone. Don't take them for granted. Keep appointments with your friends just like you would anyone else (unless of course it's an emergency). If it simplifies things, alter the location or time you're meeting but avoid canceling on them because you'll want them there for you when you need them.

Speak Up

Don't assume your friends know how you feel all the time. If something is bothering you, bring it to the table before it grows like a weed and strangles your relationship. You'll always feel better if you resolve the issue early on, and just think how much better you'll sleep at night. Go to the friend with whom you have an issue, not to other friends. All that does is circumvent the situation; it won't be solved unless you face it head-on. Keep in mind, too, that other people can misunderstand and redirect a situation in a direction you never intended. Undoing such damage is more work and more emotional than if you had gone straight to your friend in the first place. A true friend will listen and talk things out.

Praise Your Friends
Let them know how much you admire them and what they are doing. Be generous, but always sincere, with your compliments.

Hone Your Sense of Humor
Be self-effacing and always ready to laugh at yourself. Simple things, such as mispronouncing a word, that are usually embarrassing among strangers would be funny around friends so go ahead and giggle about them. If you see the humor in a situation, your friends will love you for it.

Feeding your soul with healthy, lasting friendships will provide you a lifetime of support, fun, encouragement, and emotional reward. Cultivating healthy friendships (and knowing which ones are worth holding on to for the long haul) provides you the support you'll need during trying times and appreciate during your successes.

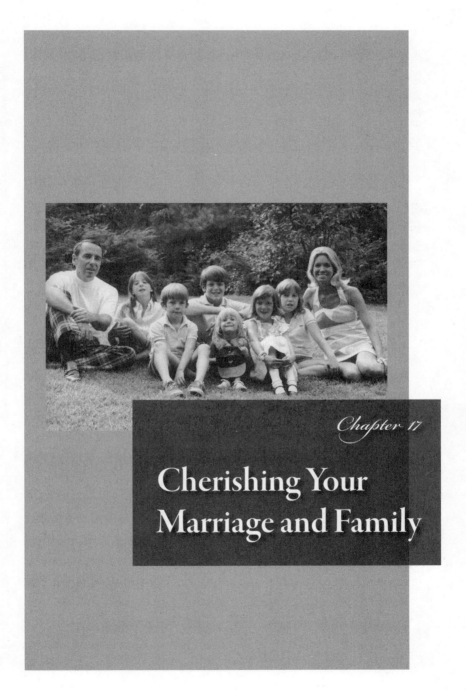

Chapter 17

Cherishing Your Marriage and Family

N o matter what you've done for yourself or for humanity, if you can't look back on having given love and attention to your own family, what have you really accomplished?

—*Lee Iacocca*

We've discussed the importance of friendships and how they add balance to our lives. This chapter is devoted to the people who are often the closest to our hearts—spouses and family. The relationships we have with our relatives can really stir up our most fundamental emotions, from delight and pride to angst and conflict. Without families, therapists wouldn't have jobs and holidays wouldn't be the same. No family is without its issues, but relatives can also be our most trusted confidants, our reasons for picking up the phone, and those we count on for acceptance more than anyone else. Immediate families are connected in ways that only the individuals involved can relate to; each family differs in the style and way members communicate, show support, raise children, and love one another. It's as though each family has its own secret language, and what makes sense for one family would make another shake its head in wonder.

Unlike friendship, marriage and family relationships are the focus of many books. They address all kinds of topics—first marriages, second marriages, and integrating children into a new home with a new spouse and frequently stepsiblings and pets. In addition to books, there are counselors and support groups for divorce, grief, parenting, sibling relationships, and other family-related issues. Because family is the core of our being in many ways, it makes sense that the resources for coping with and enhancing these relationships are plentiful.

My Story

I've had my own experience with family, so I come to you from a place of experience. A successful marriage that is still thriving and six equally successful children have given me a wealth of knowledge and wisdom to share. While we all have different perspectives and family dynamics, I cannot stress how important it is to nurture your family relationships. In some cases, close friends can become family; love of a friend can certainly be as strong as, or stronger than, love within a family. As an only child, my friends and classmates were the closest things I had to siblings, and in many ways I was as close to them as I might have been to a sister or a brother.

I've mentioned my family throughout this book but haven't yet given a clear picture of the role they play in my life. When I look back, the images I see and the stories they tell covers a wide expanse of relationships. My parents, stepparents, aunts, uncles, cousins, and grandparents all played roles of varying significance when I was growing up. That was chapter one of my life. Then along came chapter two, and I wanted to make that different. Not that chapter one was necessarily bad or unhappy—it had many wonderful components that I wanted to emulate, but it also laid the groundwork for the very different lifestyle I would later choose.

Let me draw you a mental picture of chapter one. I was born in California during World War II to an American mother, Dorothy Crispo, who had grown up in South America and moved to Pasadena for finishing school, and a father, Fred Hamlin, who had graduated from Cal Tech and become a civil engineer in the navy. Soon after they divorced (when I was four), my mother began what was to be a long and illustrious career with Pan American Airlines and Intercontinental Hotels in New York, while I went off to boarding school. She had spent her own childhood in convents in Brazil and Argentina, so the idea of her daughter following a similar course was not unusual. As it turned out, boarding school was to be a way of life for me throughout my education, even after my mother married my stepfather, a loving and beloved man whom we all called "Poppy."

Each June I jetted across the country to spend the summer months with my father and stepmother in San Luis Obispo, California, and in the fall I returned to school on the East Coast, with occasional weekends in New York. Remember what I said about each family being different in its own way? In Manhattan I had the Auntie Mame–type mother and an adorable Italian stepfather who had a voice like Pavarotti (at least to me), sang in Broadway choruses, and made the world's best lasagna and meatballs. Weekends with them were eagerly anticipated and treasured, a special party with just the three of us. Winter weekends often meant skating at Rockefeller Center, going to movies or plays on Broadway, or seeing the Rockettes at Radio City Music Hall.

Conversely, my summers in California were often tense and challenging, although not without their happy times. My father and stepmother were good people, but their personalities were entirely different from my mother's and Poppy's. My father, ever the engineer, was demanding and critical, unable to show emotion or voice approval. As often happens, he mellowed in later years, but at the time it was a very difficult environment for a sensitive young girl. Luckily, I had wonderful grandparents; an aunt and uncle who lived nearby with my cousins, three lovely girls about my own age; and a girlfriend who has been one of my closest allies since we were six. Summers meant beach parties, drive-in movies, hamburger places with waitresses on roller skates, and my first love. Over time my dad and his wife had three children, and although they were a good deal younger than I, they added many pleasant elements to the time I spent out west.

One of my fondest memories is of my grandparents taking my cousin, Sylvia, and me camping every year in Yosemite National Park. That was before it became as popular as it is today, and campers could drive in and select a prime spot in the heart of the valley along the Merced River to pitch a tent or park a trailer. Gathering each evening in Camp Curry to watch the Firefall as it spilled down the rocky cliffs from high above to the strains of "Indian Love Call" was a nightly tradition that still stands out vividly in my memory.

Those were the high points, however. I was often lonely and filled with insecurity when I was young. As I lay in bed in my dorm with five other little girls and a radio for company, I worried about my mother, who frequently flew over the Andes in small four-engine planes. I was terrified that one would crash and I'd never see her again. In school, I nervously waited for the phone to ring and her bright voice to reassure me that she was all right. When I was at my grandparents' home, there were seldom other children around, leaving the cooks and gardeners to be my friends. These scenarios were not what I wanted for my own children—not at all. I wanted to be married to a wonderful man who had the same dreams and values I did. I wanted a home filled with love and laughter and children we could shower attention on. And, most important, I wanted to be there for them. Enter chapter two.

Wally and I met at Rollins College in Winter Park, Florida, and married in New York City over Christmas vacation in 1959. Seven years older than I, Wally was ready to settle down and get on with his life. When I walked into the dining hall for dinner on my first night at Rollins, Wally spotted me and, without so much as knowing my name, turned to one of his fraternity brothers, declaring, "That's the girl I'm going to marry."

In December of '59, in the midst of a blizzard in New York City, two only-children married and began their adventure together. Family life for us has always revolved around our children, particularly when they were growing up. We had two boys and four girls in nine years, and there was never a dull moment (although there were plenty of times when I wished for one). Raising a large brood certainly was not without its challenges, but the rewards have been enormous. Family life for us meant creating our own traditions for birthdays and holidays, often including extended family members. It meant sharing the day's events around the dinner table every evening. It meant Wally coaching the children in team sports and me taking them swimming and skating. It meant special visits to see my mother ("Mima") and Poppy—first in New York City and later in Carmel, California—and spring vacations with Wally's parents in Ft. Lauderdale. It meant going to see the Mets play at Shea Stadium and picnics on the beach. It meant being together, learning about sharing, tolerance, respecting others, encouraging and supporting one another, and standing by each other through all sorts of situations. It meant learning to deal with disappointment as well as celebrating success. I don't mean to say that life was always easy or perfect. We were all human, and in many ways it was a learning game for everyone. But Wally and I gave our children the foundation of a strong family unit to fall back on, which now provides the basis for the solid connection they all enjoy today.

When friends asked us if we could ever have predicted what career paths our children would choose, Wally and I remember a day many years ago when he came home and told me about the findings of a child psychologist who had visited the school that day. Dr. Mel Levine from the University of North Carolina had spoken to the faculty and explained how children frequently show you what career they will eventually embrace by what games they play. Studies revealed that what they want to play and how they play are excellent predictors of future careers and/or pastimes. For example, Jim, now with NBC NewsChannel, used to write sports stories. He and his brother, Gus, who is with ESPN, watched baseball games on television with the audio off and used two wooden spoons as microphones to "announce" the games. Darcy was always organizing SWAT teams in the neighborhood before she went to the police academy and became a Connecticut state trooper. Annie showed artistic talent from the time she was little and is now a photographer and designer in Marin County, producing many album covers and posters for The Grateful Dead, among others. Heather loved making up short stories and anything that involved the written word. She is now my coauthor on this book and has written several others. Katy was a very strong athlete who won every award at school. She made it all the way to the finals as a competitor on "American Gladiators" and is now teaching her two children to figure skate and play ice hockey.

Now our children are all grown and off on their own. They have developed into successful, happy adults with fulfilling lives. We are still very tuned in to what they are doing and we are frequently in touch, but our relationship with them is entirely different. Our children are with us for such a short time; they are put on this earth to develop their own passions and interests and to make their own way. Wally and I strongly believe in not interfering and not offering advice unless we're asked, and we have never told them how they should live their lives. The result has been that we are close friends and confidantes to all of them, and in many ways we're having even more fun with them today than we did when they were younger.

We also have the many joys of having seven grandchildren. Every word ever written about how silly and doting grandparents can be is entirely true. We play, we snuggle, we read them stories, and we hug and kiss them until they must want to holler at us to stop.

Life for Me Now

I didn't mention my life's chapter three, but here I am in yet another phase of my journey, and it's very different from the first two. Twenty years ago, Wally and I moved cross-country from a large home that had once been filled with children to a two-bedroom condominium with just the two of us and a drop-dead view of Monterey Bay. He recently retired from teaching at the Stevenson School in Pebble Beach, which culminated a forty-five-year career. I am still very much involved with both my public relations position at Pebble Beach Resorts and, of course, modeling when the opportunity presents itself and I am able to manage it. We have each taken on new roles that are very different from the ones we started out with, and we are figuring them out and making our way through this uncharted territory day by day. With humor, open minds, and wisdom gained from so many years together, we are able to balance it all and make it work gracefully.

When people ask us what the secret to our long marriage is, we quote Ogden Nash, "To keep your marriage brimming with love in the loving cup, when you're wrong, admit it, when you're right, shut up."

Cultivating Family and Marital Relationships

There are many ways to encourage closeness among your family members. Sometimes it's the smallest acts that show the ones you love how much they mean to you.

Find Ways to Communicate Regularly

Having our family spread out on two coasts is not without its challenges and difficulties. With four children and five grandchildren on the East Coast, visits are never frequent enough and time spent together is always too short. Phone calls, e-mails, blogs, and message boards help us keep in touch. Our family has a message board on the Internet that's just for us, and it has proved to be an extremely effective way to keep in close touch. I cannot recommend it highly enough, particularly for families who are spread out around the country or the world. There are all sorts of topics on ours, anything one of us wishes to share with the others is fair game—things going on in someone's life at the moment, exciting or interesting happenings, ideas we want to bounce off one another, photos, and memories. The most interesting things of all are the old memories of family holidays in Greenwich, vacations we took together, and funny things that happened (especially amusing when it's something that Wally and I, thankfully, had no idea of at the time—oh, the things you find out when your children are grown and start reminiscing!). The family message board is a wonderful tool for keeping in close touch.

Document Your Memories
This is relatively easy to do through the written word and with photographs. In particular, digital photography has been a great blessing. Now it is so simple to take a few pictures and e-mail them or post them on one of the many excellent websites such as Kodak Gallery or Snapfish that offer all kinds of options for prints and gifts.

Cherish Family Traditions
Whether it's something as ridiculous as playing "punch buggy" with each other whenever you see a Volkswagen Beetle or something as meaningful as the special smorgasbord dinner we had on Christmas Eve when the children were little, which they now do with their families and friends, family traditions

are very important. Keeping these simple traditions alive is a good way to stay connected.

Another thing I've done is put together a family cookbook with recipes for all our favorite dishes so the children can re-create their old favorites for themselves and their families. You can make this as simple or as elaborate as you want. The idea is to have fun with it and keep memories alive.

Encourage Diversity by Keeping an Open Mind

So you don't like your sister's husband? You think your brother's children are too wild and unruly? Find ways to celebrate and praise them. Ask your sister's husband about his boring job and try to engage him. Compliment your niece on her pink hair. Make an effort to be understanding and realize that they, too, are a family unit.

Think about all of the family dynamics and combinations that are considered normal these days. It's feasible for a baby boomer to welcome a new stepparent into the fold or for a grown child to be on his second or third marriage. Some families' dynamics don't change much over the years, and others have nothing but upheaval. The ever-changing role of family constantly brings new experiences, emotions, and even disappointments. But mostly it brings new opportunities for growth and understanding.

Inspire and Support One Another

But also know when to bite your tongue. Remember that we're each starring in our own movie, and there are times when it's better (as a supporting player) to send love and let live. Your family members all have their own experiences to go through, and they might just surprise you by coming out on top.

I believe that people—especially children—are more cognizant of family situations, combinations, and permutations than ever before. They are raised to understand that the core unit of a family can be a mixture of race, religion, and gender, and that it is constantly adjusting. Half of my grandchildren have been through their parents' divorces, yet they all know they are loved by both parents and their extended family members. That's not to say these weren't difficult times for them, but they are also more aware—and more accepting—of divorce now because many of their friends are in the same situation. When my parents divorced, I was really too young to understand the ramifications, and as I grew up, none of my friends had similar experiences, so I processed it differently. As a grandparent, I've been able to relate to my grandchildren on this level, and this deepens a dimension of our relationship. All of my children were very close to my parents, and I wanted the same connection to my grandchildren.

Say "I Love You"

Once you have your own family, you can often forget to tell your original family members that you love them. Some people are more comfortable saying it than others, so if you're not prone to verbal expressions of affection, there are many ways of showing it that can be just as or more meaningful. Pick up the phone and make a call for no particular reason or send a note, card, or small gift just to let someone know you're thinking about him or her. The idea is to express love in whatever way suits you best.

Show Gratitude

Family members are often the first people you call in times of need. Show your gratitude for their support by sending a thank-you note, a gift card to their favorite store or eatery, or better yet a personal gift. Taking family members for granted can wear everyone out, so keep the favors and gratitude flowing.

Remind Your Spouse Why He Fell in Love with You

Was it your sense of humor? Your addiction to old movies? Your love of cooking? While it's healthy to grow and change, occasionally it's fun to resurrect something about yourself that your spouse first fell in love with.

So often it's not the big things that bring back a flood of memories but the silly everyday events that happen to remind you why you fell in love with each other. For us it might be something as mundane as sitting in the middle of the bed watching *Casablanca* with a plate of Poppy's spaghetti and meatballs. And here's a silly one—when I first met Wally we were in college in Florida where the humidity invariably turned my hair infuriatingly curly, a look he loved and I detested! Now that we're living on the West Coast where fog can be just as annoying when it comes to my hair, the same thing will happen and he'll get that glint in his eye that he's remembering another time, another place. We laugh over old jokes or lines that just the two of us shared when something happens to spark a memory. Silly little things in and of themselves mean nothing, but when they're shared between the two of you over the years, they keep your history alive and remind you of all you've been through together.

Remember That We're All Individuals

Realize that your little sister isn't the kid climbing a tree and scraping her knees anymore. She's a grown woman with her own dignity and pride. See and respect her as that person. Recognize your parents for the wisdom they've earned, your brother for the father that he is, and so on. Break out of the mind-set that they are all still the same as they were when you were in school, and realize that everyone has their own lives and identities.

In writing Chapter 9, I was reminded of the influence we have on so many other people's lives. We all star in our own life movie and are constantly being given opportunities and chances to better ourselves and grow. For example, coauthoring this book with my daughter provided us with the opportunity to delve into one another's lives. I was able to see and appreciate her role, challenges, and rewards as a writer, and she put the rest of her projects on hold to immerse herself in this one and to learn more about my life. She now points out to many friends and family members that you shouldn't think you know someone well, even your own mother, until you attempt to write her story from her perspective. This project served as an eye-opening experience that we both have embraced, and the rewards of working together on our unified message have given us enthusiasm and excitement. Compromise and consideration were part of the formula; in fact, when it came to writing Chapter 6, Heather stated, "You do this one, Mom. I'm not writing about your sex life!"

Releasing expectations of any sort is difficult to do when it comes to your children or spouse. Remembering that we're all here for our own journey and you can't control the paths that others may follow is critical. You can fill the role of spouse, parent, friend, and supporter at different times, but other times you have to let someone find his own way, no matter how difficult it may be—especially when you see him going down a path you don't feel is a healthy choice. Being able to recognize these times and situations, without abandoning your loved ones, is essential to maintaining your own health and the family relationships you hold dear.

Be Each Other's Best Friend

Count on one another as you would friends. When your brother confides in you, lend an ear and take it to heart by keeping his secret. You want him to do the same for you; maybe he has many times. Trust is imperative to any healthy relationship. Support your relatives through the celebrations, changes, and pitfalls while still letting them live their own lives.

Take Out the Garbage Literally and Figuratively

Helping out around the house obviously goes a long way, but learning to let go of harbored bad feelings and releasing animosities is primarily healthy for *you*. Forgiveness and letting go benefits everyone involved, and there comes a time when taking out the garbage just needs to be done or the house gets pretty smelly.

I certainly am not a psychiatrist, psychologist, or even a family therapist, and I am in no way equipped to write about other people's lives or give advice on how they should live. As I write this book, I often feel that I am sitting in my living room surrounded by friends as we have a cup of coffee and delve into all of the aspects of our lives. In many ways, this has been a very personal journey for me—another adventure I never anticipated having.

Chapter 18

Believing in
and Following
Your Dreams

D reams come true; without that possibility, nature would not incite us to have them.

—*John Updike*

Have you wished upon a star lately? Blown out birthday candles after making a wish? Shared with your best friend what you really wanted to be when you grew up? Dreams dance in and out of your mind through speech, journal writing, daydreaming, and pure vision or thought. Dreams help you make it through another day, give you something to aspire to, and challenge you. But the real challenges come after the starlit night turns to dawn, after the birthday candles melt, and after lunch or coffee with the friend is over. You've made the dream known by formulating it in your mind and expressing it in many ways. These first steps are sometimes the most courageous ones, but actually fulfilling your dreams is what makes the difference between dreamers and creators.

The exhilaration of considering a dream has been established. You've created a desire in your mind and soul, and manifesting it into the physical realm can feel real and daunting all at once. So how do you take a dream from your mind and soul and allow it to unfold into the physical? Action!

Such a simple word can leave dreamers paralyzed, but without action many dreams remain just that—dreams.

When you combine the belief that your mind and soul are in step with appropriate action, your visions become realities. Realities are formulated by the steps, decisions, and moves you make toward your dream. Sometimes they're baby steps because that's all you can do for the moment. Sometimes they entail a leap of faith that leaves you feeling as though you're floating in midair until you land smack inside your dream. Whether you need the slow and steady baby steps or the exhilaration of the leap, when you accomplish what you set out to do, the reward is the same. More commonly, the process involves the repeated ebb and flow of thought, belief, and action. You think of a step, you believe in it, and you take it. The most rewarding times are those when you become so absorbed in the process of creation that you can taste success the whole way through.

Every model who has taken that first step on a runway or in front of a camera, every photographer who has taken that first landscape or portrait photograph, every woman who has entered the working world after age fifty, every athlete who has shown up on a playing field or court, and every writer who has written the first word to their first novel was acting on their dreams. The model might have been inspired by attending a fashion show or paging through magazines. The photographer might have been inspired by an Ansel Adams or Dorothea Lange photograph. The athlete might have been inspired by going to a major league event or from playing with siblings or parents. In each case, something sparked in these dreamers that made them look inside themselves and decide they wanted to follow that dream.

Get into the Thought-Belief-Action Cycle

If you think of your dream as the equivalent of creating a painting, you know that you cannot stop at simply visualizing the painting in your head. Well, you could, but the painting would never become a reality without action. You must gather the paint, the brushes, the easel, and the canvas and bring them to your studio. Those are considered the foundation steps that indicate your intention to paint. When you're choosing your paints and brushes, it's your belief and passion that go into the selection of each color and tool. These actions plant the seeds and build excitement in your mind. When you think about your painting, consider what colors will be in it. How broad or fine will the brushstrokes be? This building of the foundation for your painting might not seem like an artistic or critical part of the process, but it is in many ways. By going through these motions, you're initiating your intention. You're preparing mentally for the challenges and joys that are ahead as you work to create the actual painting. What follows could never happen without buying the paint and brushes.

Depending on your ambition, goal or dream, you'll likely need or want to do some research, educate yourself, ask questions, and contact the types of people who will help you excel in your plan (if it involves others). These actions exemplify the brushstrokes you make as you begin painting on your canvas. It's a powerful part of the action-belief duo.

There will be times when you'll be on your way and the painting is starting to take shape, but an obstacle is thrown in your way, reminding you that the second part of the cycle is believing. Believing involves cultivating your self-talk.

Self-talk is the voice that plays over and over in your mind, and you've probably noticed that the voice can change its tune at the snap of your fingers. One minute self-talk will tell you the painting is beautiful, and you'll wonder why you haven't done this before. The next minute self-talk will doubt your color choices or technique. This is how it sends your mind conflicting thoughts that can either reinforce your beliefs or cause you to doubt your dreams. It can often conflict and confuse you if you're not aware of it.

Self-talk is your strongest collaborator during high moments, such as the excitement of having an epiphany. Your newfound idea feels so right, so real, and so within reach. All of your senses become involved—you can see yourself moving and smell, hear, and touch the image clearly. The dream is a reality in your mind. Self-talk bolsters these feelings, such as in an imaginary interview about your career as a painter. "So when did you know you wanted to be a painter?" the interviewer may ask. Your inner voice replies, "After I finished remodeling my house and needed to decorate it, I wanted a personal touch, so I thought I'd try a painting. It wasn't long before I realized how much I enjoyed the creative part of it and that I actually had talent. I'd always enjoyed going to museums and art galleries, but when I took on a project of my own and the feedback from friends and family was so positive, I could feel my spirit soar. That's when I knew it was my path." All of this signifies that you've begun to realize a dream, and the self-talk carries you along.

Self-talk can also be defeating if you're not careful. It creeps in when the lights are out and no one is around except for that little, nagging voice in your head that brings fear or doubt. Then the inner voice says, "You'll never be able to hang a painting in a gallery, let alone sell one. You're not professionally trained!" or "What if everyone was just being nice because they feel they have to be?" This is the self-talk that, if you don't pounce on it quickly, acts as an obstacle. I say *obstacle*, not a *barrier*, because obstacles can be bypassed, worked around, and dealt with appropriately. When you hear the voice of doubt and defeat, immediately consider what the opposite opinion is. If it helps, make it a game to see if you can figure out the antithesis. For example, turn "You'll never be able to hang a painting in a gallery" to "I'll be able to hang a painting in a gallery." Once that becomes a mantra, expand on it and say, "I'll be able to hang and sell several paintings in galleries all over the world." Because there are really no limitations. Ever. By shaking the doubt, worry, or fear from your mind, you'll propel your dream into existence, leaving everyone—especially you—saying, "See, I knew you could do it." (See Chapter 8 for more ideas on overcoming negative thinking.)

There are times when taking action, like buying the paint and brushes or creating the strokes, is easier than overcoming self-doubt and vice versa. But when you allow the combination of positive self-talk and action to create together, you'll have a powerful recipe for lining your dreams up right outside your door.

◦◦◦ Step Up and Take Action ◦◦◦

As mentioned earlier, taking action requires researching the steps you'll need to take in order to move toward your dream. Want to leave your nine-to-five desk job to become an interior designer? Start by researching your options for a certification program, offer to help redo your friend's house, and read up on all the related materials you can. Have you been longing to be a teacher but don't have the degree or credentials? Check out colleges and universities with programs that place "career changers" on track for teaching positions—there are many out there. By starting to take these steps, you'll advance toward making your dream a reality. If you're taking the baby-step approach, every inch forward is that much closer, and over time you'll see how the dream is taking shape.

All of our children followed their dreams and are realizing the careers and lifestyle they set out for. Our family is fortunate in that we all had clear visions of what we wanted to be and went for it. There have been some changes and shifts along the way, but for the most part, everyone has stayed the course or has seen what life has to offer next and decided whether or not to pursue it.

However, there are people who don't know what they truly want to do with their lives. You've heard the famous question "What would you be doing if money weren't an issue?" Some people simply don't know the answer to this question. Hearing this always saddens me because there is so much out there to take advantage of and to learn and do. We all have talents, personality traits, and many other things that can be rolled into a lifestyle, career, or hobby. Life is not meant to be stagnant; it's about constantly moving forward, growing, experiencing different incarnations, and believing in your ability to manifest different life experiences. It takes thought, belief, and action, but that's what we're here for, isn't it?

Now it's your turn to consider your yet-to-be-lived dreams or to move ahead with one that you are already creating. The following suggestions are meant to give you a jump-start and offer some assistance with believing and taking action.

Take a Trip Down Memory Lane

Trips are fun and the ones down memory lane can be engaging. While you're reminiscing, think about the dreams you had as a child or teenager that you didn't pursue. There's no need to limit dreams to career choices. Expand your horizons to vacations, events, education—anything. Did you want to drive cross-country and visit as many state parks as possible? Or did you want to become a chef? Many experiences that you dreamed of in your youth may be more plausible now. You can take a cooking class at night or go to a cooking school on vacation. Although you may not want a job as a chef anymore, think of all the great recipes you'll learn, the new aromas, and the people you'll meet in the process. The enjoyment alone will be worth it, and the experience may be that much sweeter than if you had done it long ago.

If you kept your journals or letters, read through them and see if anything catches your eye. Did you say that you wanted to be a writer? Consider writing for a regional newspaper, magazine, or newsletter. Join a writing group and learn how to critique other people's work, as this is a valuable way to enhance your own. If you don't want to share your work, you can still write in notebooks and journals. Was skydiving on your "someday" list? Ask a friend or your spouse if they'd be willing to jump out of a plane with you. If not, go anyway! You'll meet fellow adventurers with whom you can scream in midair as you fall thousands of feet in exhilaration and glee.

At this stage of the game, what do you have to lose by believing in and taking action toward a wayward dream?

Ask Questions

Open your journal or take out a piece of paper and ask yourself, "What makes me happy?" Jot down your answers, considering all the possibilities. If you woke up tomorrow morning with absolutely nothing to do, how would you want to spend the day? Would you paint, cook, or landscape your yard? Would you want to work on a business plan you've been toying around with in your mind?

Take a moment and ask yourself some questions about where you've been and where you want to be in a year, five years, and beyond. Make a list of all of your previous accomplishments. This will remind you of your ability to succeed. Without self-reflection, it's difficult to visualize new adventures and successes in your life, let alone allow yourself to believe in them.

Doing Is Believing

Once you start to create your next incarnation in life by taking action, you'll be amazed at how much easier it is to believe that you can get there. Sure, there might be some obstacles along the way, but remember that they're there to test your desire and belief in yourself. Dag Hammarskjöld said, "Never look down to test the ground before taking your next step: only he who keeps his eye fixed on the far horizon will find his right road." Keep your vision clear and see the obstacles as opportunities for growth, not as barriers.

When you believe in something wholeheartedly, it is that much easier to find yourself doing what it takes to create that vision. When the painter believes in her colorful canvases, it's easier for her to lift the paintbrush. Sometimes believing drives the action, and sometimes action drives the belief. The trick is to recognize along the way which one is in the driver's seat and let it lead the way, just as on a cross-country trip with a friend, you'll want to take turns at the wheel so that neither of you becomes exhausted or carsick. Believing and doing are a powerful team that works in your best interest.

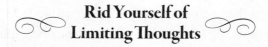

Rid Yourself of Limiting Thoughts

We live in a universe that allows for boundless opportunities and abundance in all areas of our lives. Be your own cheerleader, and when your self-talk sounds self-defeating, replace your negative words with positive ones that will support your goal and carry you through the rough patches. When you go to bed at night, it's always a good idea to make your last conscious thoughts positive, since you will be feeding your subconscious with those thoughts during the rest of the night. When you wake up in the morning, turn on the positive thoughts again—they will help drive your actions during the day ahead. While you're in the shower, make a mental list of all the successes you've had toward your goal to date and the ones that will be following that day and in the future.

If you have to, keep your goals and dreams to yourself. Sometimes sharing them with others too soon can lead to unwanted reactions of doubt and naysaying. Either don't engage others in your pursuit, or if you do and they're not supportive, just don't listen to them. Instead, take action that will show them later that you succeeded.

I'll leave you with this thought from Dr. Wayne Dyer: "Self-worth comes from one thing—thinking that you are worthy." Know that you are worthy, that you can succeed, and that anything truly is possible! Surrender control and let life surprise you.

Recommended Reading

For the Body

Making the Cut by Jillian Michaels, Three Rivers, 2008.
Mother-Daughter Wisdom by Christiane Northrup, Bantam
    Books, 2005.
Sex and the Seasoned Woman by Gail Sheehy, Ballantine
    Books, 2007.
The Wisdom of Menopause by Christiane Northrup, Bantam
    Books, 2006.
Women's Bodies, Women's Wisdom by Christiane Northrup,
    Bantam Books, 2006.
Younger You by Eric Braverman, McGraw-Hill, 2006.

For the Mind

Gift from the Sea by Anne Morrow Lindbergh, Pantheon,
    1991.
The Law of Attraction by Michael J. Losier, Wellness Central,
    2007.
The Power Years by Ken Dychtwald, Wiley, 2006.
Seeing Lessons by Tom Sullivan, Wiley, 2003.
Stand Up for Your Life by Cheryl Richardson, Free Press,
    2003.

∽❧For the Soul❧∽

The Art of Friendship by Roger and Sally Horchow, St. Martin's Press, 2006.

The Art of Living by Epicetus, HarperOne, 2007.

Eat, Pray, Love by Elizabeth Gilbert, Penguin, 2007.

The Four Agreements by Don Miguel Ruiz, Amber-Allen Publishing, 2001.

Journey to Enlightenment by Ross Bishop, Blue Lotus Press, 2008.

My First Five Husbands . . . and the Ones Who Got Away by Rue McClanahan, Broadway, 2007.

The Power of Now by Eckhart Tolle, New World Library, 2004.

A Twist of Lemmon by Chris Lemmon, Algonquin Books, 2006.

The Unmistakable Touch of Grace by Cheryl Richardson, Free Press, 2005.

Index

About the Authors

Valerie Ramsey is a sixty-eight-year-old, highly sought-after model who has graced runways, print ads, and television. She has appeared several times on "Today" and "Extra," among other shows, and has modeled for Lexus and St. John's Knits. Additionally, she is the media and public relations manager for Pebble Beach Resorts.

Valerie was a stay-at-home faculty wife and mother of six in Greenwich, Connecticut, for many years. Once her children were grown and she reached her fifties, she and her husband, Wally, moved to Monterey, California, where she worked her way up to her present position at Pebble Beach Resorts. At the seasoned age of sixty-three, she added modeling to her busy life and is represented by Ford Chicago, Look Models in San Francisco, and three other agencies. She is now a grandmother of seven (with another on its way). Valerie's website is valerie ramsey.com.

Heather Hummel, Valerie's daughter, is an author who specializes in the body, mind, and soul genre. Her published work includes "Heart Strings" in the *Blue Ridge Anthology: Poetry and Prose of Central Virginia Writers* (Cedar Creek, 2007), alongside notable authors David Baldacci and Rita Dove, and

"Signs from Mima," a featured essay in *Messages of Hope and Healing* (Sunpiper Press, 2006).

A graduate with high distinction from the University of Virginia, where she received a bachelor of interdisciplinary studies degree with concentrations in English and secondary education, Heather is currently working toward a Ph.D. in metaphysical sciences. She has completed two novels and is working on other nonfiction body, mind, and soul–based books. Additionally, Heather is a member of the International Women's Writing Guild and is a writing coach to aspiring authors. Heather lives with her two dogs and writes in Charlottesville, Virginia. Her website is heatherhummel.net.